To Tom

with Love,

Mom & Dad

Christmas 1982

Stillwater Dec 23rd 1848

W. H. C. Folsom Esqr
    Dear Sir

      Enclosed I hand you an
account of Scaling 1848 — so far
as I have Scald your average is. 406
there is about 1500 Logs below the
Falls, & mostly above Osceola not yet
scald which will be attended to, as
soon as the Ice is out — according to
the proportion of those already Scald
you will have some 30 or 40.000 feet to
add —

    I hope to make you a visit
next month. & to find you in "tall
timber" — your Logs will probably
bring 4.50 & perhaps $5 if driven
early — & there are some 24 & 32 feet
Long — a good proportion —

    Old Zack is President elect
go ahead

      Yours Respectfully

        William Holcombe

Courtesy, State Historical Society of Wisconsin.

TALL TIMBER

A Pictorial History
Of Logging In The Upper Midwest

By Tom Bacig & Fred Thompson

Voyageur Press
9337 Nesbitt Road,
Bloomington, Minnesota 55437

ISBN 0-89658-025-3

VOYAGEUR PRESS
9337 Nesbitt Rd.
Bloomington, MN 55437

Contents

Picture Sections

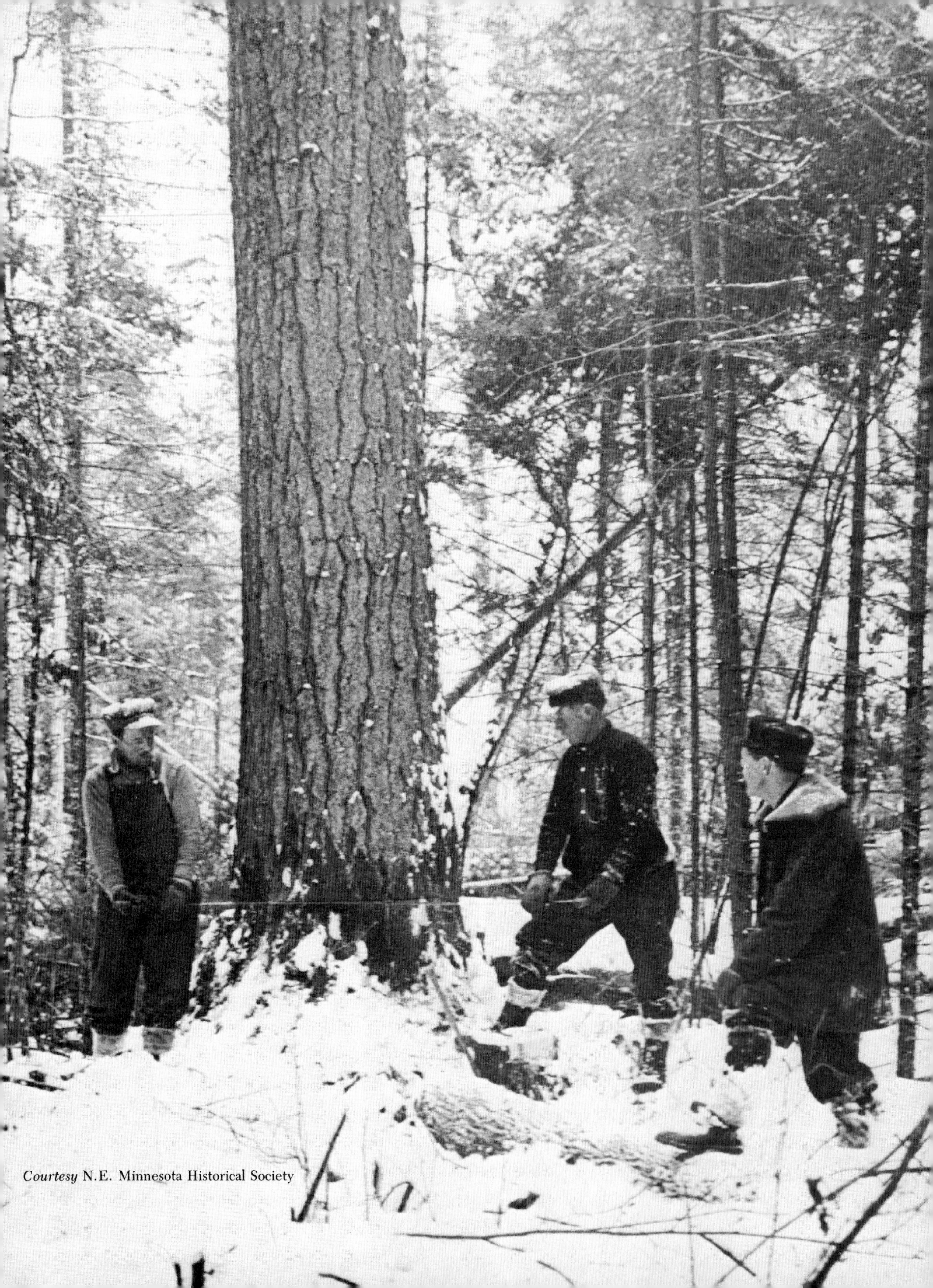

Courtesy N.E. Minnesota Historical Society

Introduction

THIS IS the story of a community of living things, a community that once contained man, and, in the way of life, has come to be contained by man.

Imagine a boundary, a point in time and space that defined the dominant period of the pines, the point when and where they had won as much of the prairie, as much of the muskeg, as much of the hardwood hills and vales as they could. Look for the shadows of that moment in the present. Like the boundaries of human communities, the boundaries of the green and growing world are often covered over as each new generation of life grows out of the decay or destruction of its predecessor. Like an archeologist, look beyond the surface and find traces. Look beyond the surface of the present; look up instead of down; look at the trees instead of the woods.

While traveling in what had been part of the pineries, seek a way to tell the story of the trees. Notice the last of them, the remnants of the community near its western edge, near one of its points of contact with prairie, hardwood forest, and muskeg. After miles of looking and thinking, the vision clears. Look above the line of birch and aspen, above spruce tips, beyond oak and maple, and see a lone, feather-branched white pine, *Pinus strobus*. Pliny the Elder spoke in Latin of its ancestors as Rome rose, "a tree in Carmenia yielding odiferous gum." Now an occasional pair of white pine stand out in the dominant growth at a point forty years past the last great cutting, past the last drive down the muddy, roiling water. These pines, grown to a cutable size, are the last standing.

Imagine the edges of the community more precisely. The first of these remaining trees, a clustering of half a dozen or more, rises above an oak and maple understory. The "overstory" is almost told, the tale of the pines almost completed. The pines stand just south of Pine City, Minnesota, a little north of Rush City, west of the St. Croix, east of the Mississippi, below the southern edge of the Hinckley fire, along I-35, north of the state's fastest growing school district; more and more people surround the pine, oak, maple, birch, spruce, aspen, play among the trees, ride up the rivers, pave the ground, choose what will grow where in prairie, woodland, pinery, and muskeg. Just beyond the trees to the east of the highway are red pines, two to three feet high. In another seventy-five years, they will form a pretty border. To the west of the highway similar borders have existed for some time, not along the highway, but behind houses, along driveways, at the edges of fields, along fence lines, or at corners. Straight lines of white pine, seventy-five to one hundred years old, mark the boundaries for humankind, the edges of the community of man.

Between the white pine by the houses and the red pine by the road lies a story. A sign announces that Pine City is the home of the Copper Tree Restaurant, an emblem of the change. Man, the mythmaker, the land changer, the most communal of all animals, has extended his community to contain the community that once contained him. This dance, this change is not new. Every species has its day, its waxing and waning, its rising and falling. Our story begins in an attempt to acknowledge this change, to shout for joy at the rise of man, the building of his farms, churches, schools, roads, bridges, towns, and cities and to weep for the fall of the trees, for the loss of the shadows, the smell, and the quiet under the trees, for the pillar shapes that inspired the Parthenon, for the mystery of their age and their ability to live beyond fourscore years, for the rusty blanket of their annual dying that rains the chemistry of life back on the soil that nurtures them. That world seemed so much theirs, so little ours. But this changing of the guard, this cycling of the species, this dance of matter from form to form, this cycle of living in dying as it was, as it is, as it shall be.

A very early view of a log jam in Aroostook County, Maine. Most of the northeast's timber resources were exhausted by the 1850's. *Courtesy, State Historical Society of Wisconsin.*

CHAPTER ONE

The Dominion of the Trees: Geological Time

IT SNOWED through the year and into the next. Sometimes it snowed large, light flakes, each leaping to its own shape as it fell, becoming a perfection of structure, a crystallization of form, an alignment of matter as exquisite as the most intricate embroidery. Sometimes it snowed heavy, wet flakes, sometimes fine hard pellets, sometimes ice motes dancing, seemingly unable to finish their fall. There were moments of bright grayness without falling snow, when the diffused light came from all directions at once. There were moments of brilliance, when the cold blue light, lined with high wisps of cloud, bounced off billions of crystal facets. But always the snow returned, building layer by layer, year after year. And this had came to pass thrice before. This fourth coming of the ice was shorter; this snowfall lasted only 75,000 years. Always before, the snow and the ice had persisted 100,000 years or more. And so it was that before the tundra and the taiga, there was ice — ice as high as 6,000 feet above the surface, mile-high ice. In the last phase, the ice sheet covered the North American continent as far south as the headwaters of the Kaskaskia River in Illinois in the west, as far south as Long Island in the east.

Against the background of these colossal changes, the dance of matter from form to form that we call life continued. Life moved with the ice back and forth across the land. Fir and spruce trees were common in Illinois and Iowa. Forest-dwelling mastodons lived in an area that stretched from Alaska to Mexico. Giant camel-llamas, giant bison, giant beaver, two species of horses, stag-moose, and caribou ranged across the continent from north to south and from east to west. Musk ox were in Kentucky, Arkansas, and Texas. Manatee sported in the waters off New Jersey; panther hunted in Alaska. And what of man? Twenty-seven thousand years ago, a man stood on Old Crow Flats at the north end of the present Yukon Territory, using a scraper made of caribou leg bone. Glaciers had lowered the sea level as they would periodically between 27,000 and 10,000 years ago, causing the Bering land bridge to appear and disappear, and across the tundra, following the animals through valleys surrounded by ice walls, came the people. Nineteen thousand years ago, they were at Meadowcroft Shelter near Pittsburgh. In 8000 B.C., there were people at the tip of South America. Eleven thousand years ago on the edge of glacial Lake Pelican in Minnesota, a fifteen-year-old girl was stabbed and her body fell or was pushed into the water. She wore as her only jewelry a conch shell from the Gulf of Mexico. In Arizona 11,500 years ago, hunters killed nine immature woolly mammoths with chalcedony-tipped lances. In 9000 B.C. at Folsom, New Mexico, a hunting party using similar weapons killed twenty-three bison. Lance points dating from around 8000 B.C. found near Debert, Nova Scotia, indicate a kill was made within fifty miles of the retreating ice, near the Bay of Fundy. As the glacier receded, humankind followed its edges and spread across the northern continent and into South America.

As the Wisconsin phase of glaciation withdrew from the vast portions of Michigan, Wisconsin, and Minnesota that it had covered 18,000 to 20,000 years ago, the tundra that prevailed along the edges of the glaciers followed its retreat. In its turn, the spruce-fir-tamarack-birch-aspen-muskeg patchwork of the taiga — the coniferous forest — followed the tundra. Finally, the mixed hardwoods moved north. At the same time, the forests continued their long war with the prairies along their western edges. Climate was the force compelling and controlling these changes. As the Wisconsin glaciation subsided, a warm, dry climate prevailed. About 11,500 years ago, most of the area that was to become the pineries was a boreal spruce forest. During the next 1,500 years, pine and hardwood forests returning from the east and south rapidly replaced the taiga. Still the

1

climate grew warmer and drier, and in some areas — the Dakotas, parts of Manitoba, Saskatchewan, Alberta, Montana, Nebraska, and Iowa — the taiga gave way directly to the advancing prairie, for during this time the community of the grasses was dominant. The tall grasses survived the drought, throve on the raging fires that swept back and forth across the grass-tree border, and began to move the trees back. Seven thousand years ago, the prairie edge stood as far east and north as it would during this recession of the ice, during the time when man entered the community of living things on this continent. But the climate changed again; it grew colder and moister. The time of the trees returned, and the taiga spread back to the west, winning back the peatlands above Red Lake and north of Mille Lacs Lake in Minnesota about 3,000 years ago. As the first English settlers landed, oak barrens claimed the Anoka Sand Plain at the western edge of the forest and formed the fire barrier that has protected the woodlands since.

One hundred years after the most recent European discovery of the New World and the first attempts at colonization in the Caribbean, no permanent posts had been established by Europeans north of Florida, and the forests contained the human communities that lived in the eastern half of North America — the woodland Indians of the North and the village people of the South. In the pineries of Michigan, Wisconsin, and Minnesota, it was the Fox, the Sauk, the Potawatomi, the Winnebago, the Menominee, the Ojibway, and along the western prairie margin, the Santee Sioux. They covered canoe and wigwam with bark from the birch tree, hunted the game that lived in the various types of woodland, picked the fruits of the deciduous trees and shrubs, and fished the waters of the great lakes, the lesser lakes left by the retreat of the ice, and the rivers and streams of the region. They dressed in the furs and skins of other woodland creatures. Their religion called for establishing harmony with the plants and animals, the hills and waters that gave them shelter and sustenance. Like all hunting nomads, the Indians lived in small groups, in rhythm with the cycle of the seasons, with the migration of the beasts of the field and the birds of the air. In fall they gathered wild rice, in spring maple sap. They fished the spawning northern, walleye, and trout as the melting snow brought them to stream and river mouths, took the migrating water birds when they could, and trapped and hunted for fur and meat. Their way of life was in and of the great trees, the wetlands, and the waterways. Further south and east, where climate permitted the growing of corn, the woodland Indians lived in villages and practiced a form of agriculture which followed the rhythms of the trees, moving their plots every ten to twenty years to allow the forest to reclaim and restore the depleted soil. This practice had been continued for centuries without disrupting the dominion of the trees.

The people of the woodland were few in number; their needs were simple . . . their way of life attuned to the harmony of the forest.

Bedagi of the Wabakanis said:

The Great Spirit is our father, but earth is our mother. She nourishes us; that which we put into the ground she returns to us and healing plants she gives us likewise.

The Winnebago of Wisconsin had a saying:

Holy mother Earth the trees and all nature are witness to your thoughts and deeds.

Tatanga Mani of the Assiniboine of Montana said:

Did you know that trees talk? They talk to each other, and they'll talk to you if you listen . . . I have learned a lot from trees: sometimes about the weather, sometimes about animals, sometimes about the Great Spirit.

Anaquoness of the Ojibway of Canada said:

To us people the woods and the big hills and the Northern Lights and the sunsets are all alive and we live with these things and live in the spirit of the woods like no white person can do. The big lakes we travel on, the little lonely lakes we set our beaver traps on, with a ring of big black pines standing in rows, always looking north, like they were watching for something that never comes, like the Indian; they are so real to us, and when we are alone we speak to them and are not lonesome; only thinking always of the long ago days and the old men. So we live in the past and the rest of the world keeps going by. For all their modern inventions they can't live the way we do and they die if they try because they can't read the sunset and hear the old men talk in the wind.

While these words come to us from a variety of cultures and in a variety of modes ranging from early Winnebago oral tradition to a 1918 Ojibway letter, they do suggest the extent to which these woodland cultures were contained by the forests that sustained them. To the Europeans who came to tame the American wilderness, such views were part of a primitive, pagan past.

According to William Bradford, the first governor of the Plymouth Colony, the first colonists to arrive in New England viewed the northern forest as a "hideous and desolate wilderness, full of wild beasts and wild men . . . the whole country, full of woods and thickets, represented a wild and savage hue." The immediate task for the colonists was to clear that desolate wilderness and to make of it a garden. The same goal carried settlers to the forests of the North and South and continues to influence settlers in northern Canada, Alaska, and even in a few woodland areas of the central region of the continent. While settlement, land clearing, and agriculture had profound effects on much of the forest land, in the pineries from the beginnings of European colonization, cutting proceeded to supply the needs of commerce. The first trees to go were the white pines over 200 feet in height, 10 feet through at the base, 300 to 400 years old. The first cuttings supplied the needs of wood-starved Europe and built the British and American fleets; the last cuttings built the midland of America and the tenements of the East. The pines were trees of destiny. Twenty yoke of oxen were required to haul a single tree from the woods during those first fellings. Special ships of the British navy, made to carry masts, took on loads of fifty timbers, one-hundred-foot columns of Maine white pine.

The demand created by the building needs of the colonies, the use of wood in wagons, boxes, and barrels, and the need to build ships for commerce and the navy produced by the Revolution and the War of 1812 was so great that what seemed an inexhaustible supply in the New England pineries was, by 1820, no longer sufficient to meet the needs of the emerging eastern urban complex of the new nation. And as the agricultural community of the new nation pushed west over the Alleghenies, the forests of New York, Pennsylvania, and Ohio fell to farm and town. As towns turned to cities, the demand for wood grew inexorably. And of all woods, the most desirable — the most malleable, the lightest, the strongest, and the best for building houses, barns, casks, wagons, furniture, and plank sidewalks — was white pine. In the East, the balance was changing. Between 1820 and 1870, the population of the United States quadrupled. The community of the trees, of the beasts of the woodland, of the Indian was giving way to the new civilization; the wilderness was becoming the garden, the garden the farm, the farm the hamlet, the hamlet the town, the town the city.

In the Northwest Territory, however, the trees still had dominion. The pines spread over areas vast, dark, green, silent; areas laced with thousands of streams; areas full of moose, deer, elk, caribou, beaver, muskrat, cougar, lynx, and wolf; areas unsettled, desolate, wild, waiting for the community of man to come to dominion. Two centuries had passed since the coming of the new way and still the slow-living, slow-growing trees had dominion. Trappers and explorers came and saw, but none conquered. There was too much of that green life to imagine the possibility of its passing. Under the pines, the needle blanket was thick; little moved. Here the trees controlled. Even the larger animals found little save shelter; food was to be found elsewhere among aspen, alder, and hazel at the edges of the bogs. In Wisconsin, Michigan, and southcentral Minnesota, shade-tolerant hardwoods, scattered white spruce, and balsam fir played the minor theme under the dominant music of the pines. In northeastern and northcentral Minnesota, balsam fir and black spruce spread under mixed stands of dominant Norway and white pine intermingled with occasional large white spruce. The symphony of the conifers seemed an eternal music, an evergreen composition that had been playing for 200 to 300 million years. Only for 130 million years had the flowering broadleafs added the fluttering notes of their variously colored appendages and the clicking of their sometimes barren branches to the rustling needle music of the high green world. Occasionally, earth, air, water, or fire had changed or moved the community. The trees had really only occupied this terrain for a few millenia, returning from a southern migration during the last long winter. Perhaps there was some warning, some change in sound, some difference in the air when the wind blew from the east. Perhaps the movements of animals, perhaps an increasing number of human visitors, perhaps the sound of steel striking wood to blaze a trail and mark a boundary, perhaps fires were more frequent and less of the music of the understory was heard. With or without warning, a new day was at hand, a new man was in the land, and the slow-growing dominants, the lordly white pine, would no longer provide the controlling themes in the woodland music. The tempo was changing and the understory was on its way to being the only story in vast areas. The pines were to learn the truth of an old saying, a commonplace of Greek or Roman wit. It is said that civilization began with the felling of the first big tree in the primeval forest and will end when the ax is laid to rest.

Homesteaders around Madison, Wisconsin, about 1873–1879. *Courtesy, State Historical Society of Wisconsin.*

(Opposite page)
Looking east and west along Superior Street in Duluth, Minnesota, one of the last major lumbertowns in the upper midwest. Circa 1890's. *Courtesy, NE Minnesota Historical Center.*

Chicago in 1858 looking southwest from the Courthouse dome. The proliferation of wooden homes and businesses in the city center explains the city's reliance on lumber from Michigan and Wisconsin and its particular vulnerability to fire. *Courtesy, Chicago Historical Society.*

Broadside advertising "Homes In Lake View Just North of the City Limits!" This subdivision preceded the area's major population growth by two years. All the ingredients of a modest income subdivision are here — the streets, subway, frame construction, schools, churches, low taxes as well as nearby industrial development and good transportation to the city. *Courtesy, Chicago Historical Society: M. B. Kenny, Printer, 1883. ICHi-06579.*

Chicago after the 1871 fire looking north, from about Congress Street, between Wabash Avenue and Michigan. *Courtesy, Chicago Historical Society.*

Black River Falls, Wisconsin. *Courtesy, State Historical Society of Wisconsin.*

CHAPTER TWO

The Rise of Man:
Immigrants and Lumber Towns

ERHAPS HUMANKIND is the latest invention of the broadleafs. After ninety million years of struggle, the conifers still dominated the world's forests; gymnosperm limited and controlled angiosperm. From the age of fishes through the age of reptiles and into the age of mammals, the dominance of coniferous plants was unchallenged. But one hundred million years ago, the flowering of the plants began, and the angiosperms, depending on the capacity of their flowering to spread themselves across time and space, engaged the battle with their self-reliant cousins. About the same time, mammals gradually began replacing the vanishing reptiles as the largest forms of animal life. The birds, the bees, passing fur bearers, and eventually, man began carrying seeds and pollen for these many-hued dwellers of the green world, and between ten and twelve million years ago, the tide turned. The plant and animal kingdoms were ruled by the newcomers. Time passed; atoms danced to new configurations. Out of the flowering trees and onto an arid plain some two million years ago stepped a near ancestor of modern man. As the great ice ages began 1,000,000 years later, *Homo erectus* was unaware that both the ice around her and the fire she had built were agents of change that would shape her and further the cause of the flowering trees. By the end of the ice ages, *Homo erectus* and her Neanderthal relatives had made way for *Homo sapiens*, and the conifers, once rulers of all, were about to discover the newest means the hardwoods had developed for taking away what remained of the kingdom of the pines.

The cradles of ancient civilization were areas where changes in climate produced optimum conditions for the development of large-scale planting and harvesting. Whether agricultural civilization first developed in China, Egypt, or Peru, it developed in a relatively treeless region. Originally, most of Europe's 2,500,000,000 acres were forested. Today, approximately 800,000,000 acres remain wooded, over 500,000,000 of these in the Soviet Union. In order for man to increase and multiply, the trees, especially the conifers, had to fall. Once the human population reached critical mass, the forests of Europe made way for the fiefdoms and farms necessary to feed the growing population. The domesticated herbivores grazed away new growth and provided milk, cheese, and meat for the burgeoning of humankind. In medieval Europe as the trees receded before the organized efforts of church and state, the way was cleared for the Renaissance and the emergence of modern European civilization. The transplanting of Europe's treeless culture to the New World is but the latest chapter in the unfolding story of man.

Predictably, as the world's forested areas have diminished, the conifers, less adaptable to the ways of man, have also lost ground to their flowery competitors. Only in the northern fringes along the edges of what remains of the glaciers does the old forest maintain its hold. There, dwarf spruce still dominates dwarf birch. Where civilization sets up its outposts, the broadleaf kingdom makes gains against the taiga and the tundra.

Since the Europeans settled in the thirteen colonies that would become the United States of America and spread across the midsection of the North American continent, over 400,000,000 of its 1,050,000,000 acres of wooded land have been cleared, and in the process, the most highly developed technological culture in the history of humankind has been built. America was built from lumber; the fuel for the melting pot, the material that made homes for Europe's downtrodden, landless masses was wood. As quickly as the settlers stepped from their ships, they took up ax and saw, set the torch to windrows and forests, and released their animals to graze. What the settlers brought to the New World was a way of life, a culture that depended on clearing land, cultivating surplus crops, and raising surplus livestock, thus creating a reserve which could support a population engaged in a wide range of commerce and industry. It began in many instances as an attempt to create new living space. Some individuals were fleeing religious or political persecution, the rigidity of European class structure, or the overpopulation of rural areas of Europe and the problems such crowding produced for peasant freeholders. Others were seeking the opportunity to improve their personal situations by escaping indebtedness, avoiding prison cells or the hangman's noose. Still others came to find adventure and profit, to free themselves from the constraints of European culture. All that stood between the settlers and realizing whatever dreams brought them to America was the forest — its trees and inhabitants. The Europeans lost no time in removing that obstacle.

Since 1631, when the first pines were milled at Salmon River Falls, South Berwick Township, Maine, Americans have been in the lumber business. Such local mills supplied the needs of growing settlements and encouraged the clearing of trees for agricultural development. Though these mills were small, water powered, and used single-blade muley saws (a long, thin-bladed saw set in a wood frame), they sprang up in every community. By 1840, there were 31,560 sawmills operating in the country, 6,356 in New York alone. Most of the New York mills were operated by men who were part-time farmers, part-time lumbermen. They cut to build the new nation's fastest growing state and could not cut enough to meet the demand. In 1850, New York led all states in lumber production; similarly, for one or two years between 1860 and 1870, Pennsylvania was the nation's leading lumber producer supplying local needs. But it was in Maine and New England that lumber was cut for export, cut to supply the insatiable demands of Europe, New York, Massachusetts, and Pennsylvania.

At first, the waters decided which trees fell and which stood. In Maine, the landlookers moved up the Kennebec, the Penobscot, and finally, the St. Croix, following the capillaries feeding these arteries to their sources in the body of the pineries. Along the streams they found the stands of pine, and looking first for the best — the tallest, straightest stands — claimed the trees for ships and cities. The trees close to the rivers were all that mattered. The only way to move the wood was to float it. In fact, one of the virtues that made pine so prized was its buoyancy. These mature white pine, trees averaging 125 to 200 feet, with trunks 2 to 10 feet in diameter, floated high during spring drives. Such trees yielded between five and nine 16-foot logs, clear and clean of knots with only a slight taper. In the pineries of Maine and New England, there was no other way to move the vast volumes of lumber that were needed to build the colonies and the new republic. But by 1836, the white pine loggers of Maine were already buying standing timber in Michigan near Port Huron. By 1840, the Maine loggers were in Minnesota and Wisconsin. What brought them west were the white pine stands close to rivers and streams. In Maine by 1840, the stands along the Androscoggin and the Kennebec had been largely exhausted. In 1839, lumbermen on the Kennebec tried to use Moosehead Lake as a means of taking logs from the upper Penobscot. Lumbermen with holdings on the Penobscot prevented them from digging the necessary canal and then proceeded, in 1841, to build a dam on the Allagash to bring the logs down the Penobscot. The white pine of Maine would continue to be logged into the 1890s, but by 1861 more spruce was being cut than pine.

In the words of Stewart Holbrook, ". . . it wasn't a dearth of timber that drove Maine men West. It was a dearth of *white-pine* timber, something vastly different in those days. When they talked about timber, by the Holy Old Mackinaw, they meant white pine." And in the Northwest Territory, what awaited these lumbermen were enormous stands of that same white pine. In Michigan, the government estimated that 150 billion board feet of white pine could be cut. By 1897, 160 billion had been cut and 6 billion were still standing, mostly in the Upper Peninsula. In Wisconsin, an additional 130 billion board feet of red and white pine awaited cutting. In Minnesota, there were 68 billion board feet. Between 1873 and 1920, the old Northwest Territory would produce 217 billion board feet of pine.

The only thing the lumbermen needed as they moved west was a market for the wood they cut. In 1833, Chicago was a community of 350 people. There were fewer than two people per square mile living north of Lansing in Michigan, north of Madison in Wisconsin, and west of the Mississippi in Minnesota and Iowa. The population of Ohio, Indiana, and Illinois, while greater, was still sparse. No community west of Detroit, except St. Louis with a population approaching 10,000, had more than a few thousand inhabitants. West of the Mississippi and north of the Missouri, the only settlement was at Iowa City. But the Erie Canal opened the way west and the movement of people began.

During the 1820s, approximately 10,000 immigrants a year entered the United States. Between 1830 and 1840, an average of 54,000 Irish, German, and English settlers and laborers came annually to build the canals and railroads that would carry them and succeeding generations west and to establish their settlements at the railheads and on the prairies. During the next ten years, 1,620,000 more immigrants came, and 2,814,554 came between 1850 and 1860. These immigrants came, like those who had come and would come, with dreams; dreams as various as the immigrants themselves, but always with dreams of the land. Hector St. Jean Crevecour, one of the earliest European observers of this immigration, explains with precision and elegance the forces that drove this stream of flesh.

> In this great American asylum, the poor of Europe have by some means met together, and in consequence of various causes; to what purpose should they ask one another what countrymen they are? Alas, two thirds of them had no country. Can a wretch who wanders about, who works and starves, whose life is a continual scene of sore affliction or pinching penury; can that man call England or any other kingdom his country? A country that had no bread for him, whose fields procured him no harvest, who met with nothing but the frowns of the rich, the severity of the laws, with jails and punishments; who owned not a single foot of the extensive surface of this planet? No! urged by a variety of motives, here they came. Every thing has tended to regenerate them; new laws, a new mode of living, a new social system; here they are become men: in Europe they were as so many useless plants, wanting vegetative mould, and refreshing showers; they withered, and were mowed down by want, hunger, and war; but now by the power of transplantation, like all other plants they have taken root and flourished! Formerly they were not numbered in any civil lists of their country, except in those of the poor; here they rank as citizens. By what invisible power has this surprising metamorphosis been performed? By that of the laws and that of their industry. The laws, the indulgent laws, protect them as they arrive, stamping on them the symbol of adoption; they receive ample rewards for their labours; these accumulated rewards procure them lands; those lands confer on them the title of freemen, and to that title every benefit is affixed which men can possibly require.

The landless came to the land. The dominion of man came to the woodlands of the pineries of North America driven by the highest aspirations of the species and found in the green and growing woodlands the material to build a nation of free people. To fail to understand the dreams of these migrants is to fail to understand what must be celebrated in the passing of the pines; for as surely as the beauty, silence, and grandeur of primal forest passed with the trees, the greatest age of freedom and prosperity the human species has known came as the trees fell.

At first in Michigan, Wisconsin, and Minnesota, the volume of the cutting was small as the settlers cut only what had to be cut to clear farmland, build their farms, make their furniture, fence their land. As long as the settlers had to carve the farms out of the woodlands, the cutting of the white pines of the Midwest went slowly. But as the tide of immigrants flowed out of the woodlands into the grasslands of the Midwest, immense quantities of lumber needed to be moved enormous distances to supply an ever-increasing demand. In 1847, the clear cork pines of Michigan began to float down the Cass, the Shiawassee, the Flint, the Tittabawassee, to the Saginaw, through the mills across Lake Huron, Lake Erie, and Lake Ontario to Tonawanda, New York, and finally, through the Erie Canal to Albany, New York. For in spite of enormous numbers of migrants moving west, the population of the East and its centers of commerce continued to grow rapidly. As humankind flowed west, the wood flowed east, south, and west. It built the cities and towns that sprang up along the shores of Lake Erie; and throughout Indiana and Ohio, mansions, shanties, churches, saloons, barns, and outhouses of Michigan white pine sprang into shape. The green gold flowed down the Muskegon on Michigan's western shore and across Lake Michigan to Chicago. Michigan pine would divide the Illinois prairie and build the Midwest's largest city — houses, stockyard pens, granaries, mills, and all. And from Minnesota and Wisconsin down the St. Croix, the Chippewa, the Wisconsin, the Black, and the Mississippi, white pine came to St. Louis. From St. Louis it would move as far west and south as Oklahoma, as far west and north as the Yellowstone. Michigan pine built Chicago, Pittsburgh, and Albany. Minnesota pine was sold in Winnipeg and built the oxcarts that carried the farmers to Manitoba's prairies. After the 1871 fire, pine from Wisconsin and Michigan's Upper Peninsula rebuilt Chicago.

And as surely as the pine built the cities, towns, hamlets, and farms of the Midwest, it was the lifeblood of the emerging economy of America's midlands. The cutting of the trees moved Eastern capital and loggers to the West to supply the sodbusters, who in turn supplied the lumbermen with their produce. The towns of St. Louis and Chicago turned into cities by selling lumber to the settlers; the settlers sold their produce to the townsmen who made the wagons, barrels, plows, shovels, and axes needed to plant more wheat, barley, corn, and rye to feed a nation whose population was exploding. From Chicago and St. Louis, rail lines began to stretch north, south, east, and west, and more wood and wheat moved in all directions. Between the Alleghenies and the Rockies, across the Mississippi Basin, white pine lumber created the merchandising and transportation centers of the Midwest. Chicago and St. Louis became the first major lumber markets in the heartland; later they became major transportation and farm produce centers.

Perhaps no mid-American metropolises owe more to this flow of living wood, this final exchange between the pineries and the prairie, than do Minnesota's Twin Cities — Minneapolis and St. Paul. Situated on both sides of the Mississippi near its junctions with the Minnesota draining prairie lands and the St. Croix draining pineries, Minnesota's largest communities grew out of the exchange of wood and wheat, out of the breaking of sod and the cutting of trees, out of the rich loam of the Red River Valley, out of the sloping pine-covered valleys of the Rum and Snake rivers, out of the ancient struggles between ice and rock, between grass and trees, between needles and leaves, between cones and flowers. The settlement began in 1819 with the cutting of pine to build Fort Snelling where the Minnesota River met the Mississippi. A government-operated sawmill was established at St. Anthony Falls on the Mississippi to saw boards for further construction at the fort and at *Innijiska*, White Rock Landing, the present site of the city of St. Paul. The land for the fort, the sawmill, and the landing had been purchased from the Sioux for sixty gallons of whiskey and some "presents" fifteen years before by Zebulon Pike at Thomas Jefferson's order. The chief purpose for constructing the fort and landing was to provide a base for controlling fur trade in the region. The first steamboat arrived at the landing in 1823. The community spread slowly along both sides of the Mississippi between the fort and the landing. Governor Dodge of Wisconsin Territory made a treaty with Ojibway of Minnesota and Wisconsin in 1837 for purchase of the land between the Mississippi and the St. Croix. Previously, the westernmost provinces of the dominion of the pines had not been open for large-scale lumbering operations on any legal basis. Some settlers had, of course, made cuttings, and a few enterprising lumbermen had contracted with Ojibway bands along the St. Croix and Snake rivers to cut timber and build mills on their lands. Two years after the treaty was ratified, the first commercial sawmill in the area was operating at Marine on St. Croix northeast of White Rock Landing.

At the time, there were two hundred settlers at White Rock Landing; most were French and lived by fishing, hunting, and trading for furs. In 1841, Father Lucien Gaultier arrived to guide these settlers in building St. Paul's Church of white pine logs on the bluff above the landing, and White Rock became St. Paul's landing. Ninety-five boats docked at St. Paul's Landing in 1849, and the village of thirty-two houses was designated the capital of the new Minnesota Territory. The boats carried men and supplies for the logging operations spreading north along the St. Croix and the Mississippi. A new treaty negotiated with the Sisseton and Wahpeton Sioux in 1851 opened up prairie land along the Minnesota River and the Red River in the north for settlement and farming. Two years later, the rail link between Chicago and New York was completed; immigrants from Ireland, Germany, Norway, and Sweden arrived in Chicago and traveled by steamboat upriver to St. Paul. Over a thousand boats docked at St. Paul in 1858. The boats were fed by three new railroads and brought an ever-growing stream of settlers to the new territory. The population of Minnesota Territory jumped from 6,000 in 1850 to 40,000 in 1855 and 150,037 in 1857. There were so many immigrants in St. Paul that tents were set up in the streets to house them. As the new decade began, farmers came to St. Paul bringing their wheat to market and buying the lumber they needed to build their farms. The first Twin was born as a port of entry to pinery and prairie.

As the new settlers began producing foodstuffs and building their barns and houses, lumbering in the region escalated. It was possible to put more and larger crews into the woods because supplies could be purchased locally and transported shorter distances. The homesteader who came to sow in spring, cultivate in summer, and reap in fall, turned to felling pine in winter. The pine heard the sound of shouts in English, French, Swedish, and Norwegian. White pine cut north of St. Paul on the St. Croix flowed south to a host of points along the Mississippi stretching through Minnesota, Iowa, and Illinois, ending at St. Louis. Pine floating down the Mississippi stopped at the mill built in 1848 at St. Anthony. Around that mill, the city of Minneapolis exploded into existence. In its first year of operation, the mill cut 15,000 board feet of white pine a day. Everything cut went to local markets in St. Paul or west to the prairies. The following year, two additional mills were built. In the next seven years, five more mills were making logs into lumber at St. Anthony Falls. The mills at St. Anthony were producing 60,000,000 board feet a year for local consumption. At the same time, the waters of the Mississippi were diverted through millraces to grind wheat coming from settlements as far north as St. Cloud and as far south as Mankato. Farmers camped on Nicollet Island below the falls and waited for their wheat to be ground. By the end of the decade, 200,000 barrels of flour were produced in a single year. Ten years later, 6,998,830 barrels of flour had been ground by the Father of Waters. The second Twin was born in clouds of chaff, in the turning of millraces and the howl of muley saws, circular saws, and gang saws.

As white pine lumbering built the major market centers along the Mississippi and the Great Lakes from Albany to St. Louis, it also built the lumber towns from Maine to Minnesota, from Bangor to Duluth. The history of these communities emerges from the advance and retreat of ice and woodlands over the eons. Almost always the logging towns grew up on the waterways formed as the ice retreated. The waters rippled through adjacent stands of white pine and connected to waterways that carried the logs or milled lumber to the waiting immigrants, to the boatyards, to the farm markets, to the emerging cities. During the century when white pine lumbering was a way of life, these communities rose to supply ever-increasing quantities of pine logs and lumber; faded to cutting red pine, spruce, and hemlock; and finally became "legendary" lumber towns when lumbering gave way to logging pulpwood for paper mills or disappeared altogether. With the passing of the pines, the newly rich and, slowly, the sons and daughters of immigrants experiencing the prosperity dreamed of by their forebears came to hunt and fish, to swim, to look, to imagine what had been by peering at faded photographs in the local historical society display. The glory of the spring log drives, the sounds of the saws, the mountains of sawdust, the shouts and laughter of the crews outfitting, the coming and going of the cruisers, sawyers, swampers, teamsters, and riverhogs were gone forever. Logging continues in some areas, but lumbering has passed with the dominion of the pines. Logging now is a matter of machines — chain saws, tractors, and trucks — not of ax, crosscut, and pike; of muscle and bone; of corks, boiling rapids, and jams. The natural succession of the broadleafs brought a new community of man, a natural succession of another sort. Farewell shantyboy. Hail and well met gyppo, tie hacker, and pulper.

It was the hand-to-tree nature of early logging that fired the imagination of the young nation and made the logging towns symbols of the advance of civilization and, ironically, homes for the civilization-hating, no-holds-barred man among men, archetype of the new nation — the lumberjack. Even the greatest naturalist-environmentalist of the nineteenth century, Henry David Thoreau, sang the praises of the lumber towns and the lumbermen.

> There stands the city of Bangor, fifty miles up the Penobscot, at the head of navigation for vessels of the largest class, the principal lumber depot on this continent, with a population of twelve thousand, like a star on the edge of night, still hewing at the forests of which it is built, already overflowing with the luxuries and refinement of Europe, and sending its vessels to Spain, to England, and to the West Indies for its groceries, — and yet only a few axe-men have gone "up river" into the howling wilderness which feeds it. The bear and deer are still found within its limits; and the moose, as he swims the Penobscot, is entangled amid its shipping and taken by foreign sailors in its harbor. Twelve miles in the rear, twelve miles of railroad, are Orono and the Indian Island, the home of the Penobscot tribe, and then commence the batteau and the canoe, and the military road; and, sixty miles above, the country is virtually unmapped and unexplored, and there still waves the virgin forest of the New World.

This "star on the edge of night" gateway to "the howling wilderness" would in less than a century be crowded with caps and gowns, lab coats, surgical greens, and an occasional pair of sawdust- and oil-coated coveralls. Gone the mackinaw, the gray pantaloons, the red flannel shirts, the wool caps, the corks.

Bangor's first settler cut pine for his cabin in 1769, and a year later a sawmill was operating. Sixty-five years later, Bangor was the lumber capital of the new nation.

As Stewart Holbrook, the leading historian of Maine lumbering, points out "Bangor was the first city of size whose entire energies were given to the making and shipping of lumber and to the entertainment of the loggers who cut the trees." It now contains a group of statues "depicting three caulk-booted figures, two with peavey in hand." It is titled *The Last Drive*, and it would fit in many other squares in what was once the trackless forest, the dominion of the pines.

Saginaw, Michigan, began as a fur trade center for the American Fur Company, but by 1832 there was a sawmill operating — a steam-powered mill that could cut 2,000 board feet of lumber in twelve hours. Like Bangor, Saginaw was located on a waterway draining large white pine reserves. The Saginaw River was fed by ten rivers with 839 miles of water to float pine — the Cass, the Flint, the Shiawassee, the Bad, the Tittabawassee, the Chippewa, the Pine, the Salt, the Tobacco, and the Cedar. At first the flow of pine logs was slow. The market for the Saginaw pine lay to the east, and until the pine in Maine and upper New York was cut, most of the Saginaw pine went for local consumption. Saginaw's second mill was selling pine in Detroit by the middle of the 1840s. Five mills were operating in 1847, and a shipment went east to Albany. A New York businessman characterized the situation in the following terms.

> "A few years of continuous cutting (in Maine and New York) will demonstrate that the next generation will have to face a serious question, that of timber supplies, and whoever holds good pine lands in Michigan ten years from now, that have been purchased at present rates will have the most valuable territory in the state.

Eighty-three mills processing 41,000,000 logs were operating in the Saginaw Valley by 1869. Six thousand lumbermen were in the woods and three thousand worked the mills. The peak production year for the Saginaw Valley mills was 1882. In that year, twenty-seven major mills at Saginaw and thirty-five at Bay City cut a billion board feet of pine and shipped it east. As in Bangor, the massive volume of logs needed to meet the demand for pine filled the Saginaw and its tributaries from bank to bank. The thousands of lumbermen working for the sixty-two mills needed some system of keeping track of each company's logs. The first of Michigan's boom companies was organized to sort and raft logs for delivery to appropriate mills. Modeled on the Penobscot Boom and booms in Minnesota, the boom at the junction of the Tittabawassee and the Saginaw was the first step in organizing logging on the Saginaw so the enormous output of the 1870s and 1880s would be possible. It was also in the Saginaw region that the first of Michigan's logging railroads opened up the pines that lay between the watery fingers of the Saginaw's drainage basin. The Flint and Pere Marquette bisected the Michigan logging country and opened up vast new stands of pine remote from the rivers flowing to either shore. Thus was begun a process that by 1887 would build eighty-nine logging railroads with nearly 650 miles of track, 127 locomotives, and 2,573 logging cars. And as the steel and steam carried these remote pines to the mills, the total number of sawmills in the central portion of Michigan, an area including both the Saginaw and Muskegon operations, had fallen from a high of nearly 700 in 1873 to approximately 250 in 1885. Two years later, Saginaw firms were moving to Duluth, Minnesota, to cut the last of the pine in the Lake States. The mills in Saginaw continued to saw hardwood, hemlock, and spruce, but as in Bangor, the end was in sight. A way of life, a breed of men, a struggle between pine and oak, birch and aspen was finished in the valley of the Saginaw. In the wake of white pine lumbering, pulp and paper, salt deposits, coal deposits, oil deposits, and an emergent farming community transformed Saginaw into a town very different from Bangor. It was not the first or the last time that the emerging civilization of the New World found that a combination of glacial action and earlier geological activity forming the earth's crust placed a pine woods on top of mineral deposits. In Michigan's Upper Peninsula and in northeastern Minnesota, miners and loggers joined hands to find the raw material the emerging nation needed to fuel and build itself. The passing of the pines and the coming of the new age of man were as interwoven as the movements of ice, magma, and taiga that made the pineries and the Canadian Shield.

Located thirty miles below the edge of the pineries at the junction of the Black River, the LaCrosse River, and the Mississippi River, LaCrosse, Wisconsin, seemed to be too far from the pine forests to be a lumber town, but the rough water between Black River Falls and the junction of the Mississippi at LaCrosse made splinters of much of the lumber sawed by Black River Falls mills, and as soon as the lumbermen of the Black River area decided it was more economical to float the logs to La-Crosse, the village became a lumber town. Eventually LaCrosse mills would cut lumber from both the Black and the Chippewa basins, and the city would become a rail center, a boat-building center, and a point of entry for the immigrants who would settle Minnesota and Wisconsin. As early as 1839, a mill cut Black River pine for the first settlers. There were eleven mills on the Black River four years later. The first mill built in LaCrosse was steam powered and represented the first step in mechanizing the lumbering of the Black River region. During the fifties and sixties, the LaCrosse mills were, relatively speaking, small-capacity operations employing from eight to eighteen men. Their cut ranged from 15,000 to 50,000 board feet per day, but by 1869 over 20,000,000 board feet of lumber had been produced and production leapt to new highs during each of the next

three decades. Between 1890 and 1899, 178,000,000 feet of white pine lumber poured out of thirty-two mills from Onalaska on the northern edge of the LaCrosse area to Isle LaPlume at the southern end of the community. Rotary saws and gang saws whined through logs and the millhands worked to build the lumber rafts. LaCrosse sent football fields of Wisconsin pine south and west to build the prairie communities and to house the Germans, Norwegians, and Swedes who were settling the breadbasket of the new nation. At the turn of the century, 1,785 employees earned their livings making lumber. Four years later, there were only forty workers. But LaCrosse didn't decline with its lumbering. Moving wood had created a transportation center, and as lumbering faded, grain milling, farm shipping, breweries, agricultural implement plants, foundries, machine shops, and cigar factories survived the fall of the pines. The lumber had brought the people with their willing hands and strong backs. And so another fur traders' landing, Prairie Lacrosse, named for the ball game the Sioux warriors played on its grasslands — another point where prairies met pine — came under the dominion of man; another star was born, and the night receded north and west.

The last "star on the edge of night" in the pineries flared in Duluth. The first settler in Duluth crossed the St. Louis River from the community of Superior, Wisconsin. That portion of Minnesota Territory lying between the uppermost reaches of the Mississippi and Lake Superior, along either side of the Laurentian Divide, drained by the Cloquet, the St. Louis, and a multiplicity of short rivers with steep gradients along the north shore of Lake Superior, was Indian land. The LaPointe Treaty of 1854 opened the way for the coming of the new man to the last of the old trees. And as the era of white pine lumbering drew to a close, the newest type of lumberman came to Duluth to cut and mill white pine logs. Shortly after the LaPointe Treaty was signed, two mills were built in Oneota along the St. Louis River below the bluffs that mark the shore of Lake Superior's glacial ancestor. They cut boards for what promised to be the "Chicago of the North" and prepared for the boom that the railroads would bring. When a financial panic dashed hopes in the late 1850s, two of the early lumbering families, the Merritts and the Mungers, held on, fearing that progress had passed them by. But European civilization was on the move, and it needed wood and iron, white pine and hematite. And so it came to pass that Jay Cooke, Philadelphia banker and founder of what would become the Northern Pacific Railway, pushed rails north to Lake Superior and announced his plan to turn his line west through hundreds of miles of uncut pinery and thousands of miles of unsettled prairie. The Northern Pacific would be "the road to ride," and it would bring the wheat-wood exchange to an emerging inland port, run rails to the Pacific, prepare the way for Fredric Weyerhaeuser and syndicate, and make the great leap from white pine to Douglas fir, from lake to ocean, a leap that ended the dominion of the pines and fully established the dominion of man. Jay Cooke saw it all. He planned the production of "ready-cut" houses to shelter the immigrants on the land they purchased along the railroad right-of-way. The immigrants would pay by shipping their wheat east to Duluth for milling and down the lakes to feed the industrialized Northeast.

As the seventies began, Duluth grew in six months from a community of less than 100 to a community of 3,500. Maine lumbermen, pursuing the pines west, refitted one of the mills built in the 1850s and cut "clear lumber, dressed flooring and siding, dimension lumber, shingles, lath, door and sash" for the local community. After the planing mill, cabinetmaking and wagon building followed almost immediately. The boom was underway; its markets local, its hopes global.

As the rails for the Northern Pacific reached the Red River Valley and prairie wheat was on its way to be stored in elevators built of white pine at Duluth, the story of the lumber town was about to be told for the last time in the pineries. But the story had new dimensions. For the most part, the earlier lumbering operations in Michigan, Minnesota, and Wisconsin had been carried on by individual entrepreneurs, rugged yankees from Maine, New York, and Pennsylvania who cruised the timber, found enough capital to build a mill, and pulled themselves out of the shanties into the front office. As often as not, they could swing an ax or use a pike as well as many of their workmen. But in the Duluth area, while a generation of Maine men from the Saginaw moved west with the pine and while some leap-frogged from New Brunswick, Quebec, Nova Scotia, and Maine, it was the syndicates and the supercapitalists that would write the final chapter in the story of the pines. Fredric Weyerhaeuser and Andrew Carnegie. Names to conjure with in the "land of opportunity." These captains of industry would build their empires out of the rocks and trees of the Duluth district.

Some local lumbermen named Merritt would find during their cruising expeditions vast iron ore deposits under pine stands, capitalize a railroad to bring wood and iron ore to Duluth by borrowing from Carnegie and Rockefeller, lose everything they had in a panic engineered by the Carnegie-Rockefeller cartel, and watch United States Steel grow out of the white pine cut by its Oliver Mining Division on the lands that covered the rich ore deposits of Minnesota's Mesabi Range.

Fredric Weyerhaeuser, as a boy of seventeen, had emigrated from Germany only four years before he arrived in Rock Island, Illinois. There he began as an employee in a lumber and grain business and twenty years later began to buy logs experimentally in the Chippewa

district of Wisconsin. He was operating two mills in Rock Island in 1870 when a booming company supplying those mills with logs got into financial difficulties. Weyerhaeuser formed a syndicate to operate the boom and assure his supply of logs. As the decade of the eighties began, the Mississippi River Lumber Company and Weyerhaeuser controlled enormous areas of land, equipment, and capital, had working arrangements with the burgeoning railroads, and owned a major portion of the largest remaining stands of white pine along the Mississippi and its tributaries in Minnesota and Wisconsin. And as lumbering became more dependent on railroads, as stands of trees far from streams that could support spring drives became the only stands containing white pine, it was lumbermen with access to such capital who were able to continue lumbering. In the mid-nineties, Weyerhaeuser moved into Cloquet, upriver on the St. Louis from Duluth, acquiring six sawmills from independents who had been successfully lumbering in the area. Each of the mills owned "township after township of white pine," millions of acres, ninety-five percent of which contained white pine.

Of course there were occasional local success stories by the score. A timber cruiser named Alworth from Saginaw, Michigan, began buying Minnesota timberlands for Saginaw lumbermen in 1875, just as the Weyerhaeuser Timber Company would begin doing in the Pacific Northwest a decade later. As payment for his work, his firm gave him timberland on the Mesabi, and beneath the overburden of pine and duff lay a mountain of iron ore. But in the main, it is associations of lumbermen from Michigan, Wisconsin, and Minnesota who controlled the final stands of pine. With capital from New York, Detroit, and Chicago, they built rail lines east through northern Wisconsin to Michigan's Upper Peninsula, north and west to Winnipeg and the Canadian prairie, north to the Mesabi and iron, west to the Dakotas and wheat; and off each of these main lines were logging spurs where steam jammers loaded the logs that horses and steam haulers brought to the landings. Where there was water, the $13-a-month logger Wellington Burt could rise to being a lumberman of importance, governor of the state, and entrepreneur in the new territory of Minnesota — the American self-made man. Where steel had to be laid to get to logs, eventually the Weyerhaeuser and Rockefeller syndicates controlled.

Duluth lumber began by flowing west with the Northern Pacific, following Jay Cooke's plan, a plan developed by Philadelphia banking interests. It ended by flowing east, controlled by Michigan timber interests or Cleveland and Pittsburgh steel interests; it flowed to Tonawanda, New York, the greatest white pine assembling and distributing market on the continent, Buffalo, and Albany. From Tonawanda, the Duluth district pine left as barrels traveling to the Indies and South America and returned carrying molasses and sugar. Duluth pine built mansion and tenement to house the wealthiest and most prestigious of America's nouveau riche at the turn of the century and the immigrants of New York, Boston, Philadelphia, and Detroit. Enormous volumes of logs were rafted, pulled by powerful tugs down the north shore of Lake Superior to Duluth; lumber moved by barge and steamer down the lakes, by rail south, east, north, and west. Between 1897 and 1906, Duluth mills shipped 3,707,000,000 feet of lumber. As early as 1902, Duluth mills were beginning to run out of log stock, and by the end of the second decade of the new century, lumbering had passed from Duluth. With the closing of the Scott Graff Mill in 1932 after seventy-five years of operation, sawdust gave way to the red dust from iron ore; the smell of fresh cut wood gave way to the sulfurous smells of paper mills; lumber docks gave way to ore docks. The waterway was there; the elevators had been built; the railroads ran to the prairies; the dominion of man was at hand; the night of the old wilderness was gone, apparently, forever.

For as the trees fell, even in the areas where farming was not possible, the settlers came and stayed. Though the peopling of the pineries happened in a variety of ways, the farther from the advancing edges of farmland, the deeper into the old woods the cutting went, the more likely it was that a milling town would spring up to supply local settlers, or in the later stages of lumbering to supply white pine to towns and farms lying farther west on the rail lines that were stretching themselves across the prairie. As long as sawing large volumes of wood depended on water power or water transport, it was easier to take the logs to the milling centers at Duluth, LaCrosse, or Saginaw, but as steam-powered saws became more portable and rail lines made transport of logs more expensive than transport of milled lumber, new communities appeared in the remotest corners of the pineries.

Even in the earliest stages of lumbering, small milling communities sprang into existence and, in areas where farming was either unprofitable or extraordinarily difficult, passed into a state of suspended growth providing homes for lumbermen who worked elsewhere and entertainment centers for those living in larger communities nearby. Marine on St. Croix is a perfect example. The first commercial sawmill in Minnesota was built there in 1840 by Orange Walker of Marine, Illinois. Born in Vermont in the year of the Louisiana Purchase, Walker, had come west to Illinois and turned north to lumber on the St. Croix. With various partners, he would conduct a lumber business in Marine mills for the next forty-eight years. He would also build a town. Walker would serve as postmaster for twenty-five years and, for a short time, as a state legislator. Because the people who came to work at his mill constituted the first white settlement in

Minnesota and because all his employees needed supplies, he opened the first store in the region, and in the mid-fifties began operating a mill to supply flour for employees. But because the lumbering business in the region was soon to be dominated by Stillwater to the north, where a booming operation would develop, and Minneapolis-St. Paul to the south, where transportation, lumbering, and grain milling would become a way of life, Marine, located in a narrow portion of the St. Croix Valley far from good farmland, remained a one-mill town, contributing lumber and logs to the volumes flowing downriver so long as the Walker firm could cut or buy logs. For many years, the boom at Stillwater, which Walker had helped to organize, accomplished exactly that purpose. Walker, with his partners Judd and Veazie, rafted 8,443,680 board feet of logs at the St. Croix Boom in Stillwater during 1883. By the turn of the century, however, some logs were being towed upstream from the St. Paul boom on the Mississippi to supply St. Croix lumbermen, and as the second decade of the new century opened, milling on the St. Croix ceased. Marine survived as a recreation area for the nearby Twin Cities of Minneapolis and St. Paul, becoming a bedroom community for its ever-growing neighbors.

Hermansville on Michigan's Upper Peninsula is coming to another kind of end. Hermansville's founder fled the political and religious upheavals of Germany in the late 1840s. C. J. L. Meyer left Chicago in the mid-fifties to start a woodworking shop in Fond du Lac, Wisconsin. He began making wheelbarrows, ironing boards, doors, and sash. The Chicago fire in 1871 created a demand for materials produced at the surviving planing mill and lumberyard Meyer had built in the Chicago area. As long as the Wisconsin pine in the Lake Winnebago region lasted, Meyer was on his way to making a fortune. But the supply was dwindling, so Meyer sent forth his landlookers, his timber cruisers. The cruisers found Meyer his pine in Menominee County, Michigan, in cutover country where patches of pine remote from streams were in good supply. One damming operation had made it possible to float logs by way of the Little Cedar River to the landing that was to become the village of Hermansville. For a few years the river brought some pine to the mill, but it wasn't until the Chicago and Northwestern ran its tracks through the 50,000 acres that Meyer owned and, eventually, moved his mill over its shining rails from Fond du Lac to Hermansville that his problem was solved. Wisconsin Land and Lumber's Pine Mill Number One began sawing as the seventies became the eighties. The town was named for Meyer's son Herman. Ten years later, the Soo Line ran its tracks to Hermansville. The wood for the mill was first supplied by ice road and sledge, but shortly a tram railway with cup-wheel cars that ran on pole rails was introduced, and early in the 1880s the Hermansville and Western began hauling logs. By the mid-nineties, the pine was gone; but hardwood milling to produce flooring continued to produce excellent income for the residents of Hermansville for another fifty years. Boardinghouses gave way to permanent homes; farms were started on cutover lands; stores, churches, and schools were built; eventually the mills closed; schemes to develop resorts on cutover lands failed; and in 1948 Stewart Earle, last grandson of Meyer, began disposing of company holdings. The last two employees of the Wisconsin Land and Lumber Company — an aged watchman and grounds keeper and a 50 year old secretary — live in a near-deserted Michigan village, presiding over four rooms of a Victorian office-home of twenty rooms that was and is the glory of Hermansville, over an enormous walk-in safe containing company records and photo albums, over ten other empty buildings and a millpond turned lake. There are displays in glass cases of tools, photos, and models. Through office windows one can see an array of enormous sheds and mill buildings, all empty. There is period furniture; there are desks full of the necessary articles for conducting a business. There is a faint hope that all of this will be preserved, as if all of this is somehow the memorabilia of the passing of a race of giants; which it is. The dominion of man sometimes seems as passing as the dominion of the pines.

And west five hundred miles at the grand rapids of the Mississippi, the last of Mississippi lumber towns thrives. Here the pineries built Grand Rapids, Minnesota. Len Day came north from Minnesota's Rum River pinery. On the Rum, he lost the stake he had earned by logging in Maine. The raging Rum washed away a season's work. He got a new stake, bought timberland in the Lake Pokegama region, found iron ore on his land, and he and his sons became the chief lumbermen of Grand Rapids. There were others, of course, who cut the Pokegama pine in Itasca — Al Nason, the strongest man ever to come to Pokegama country, a Paul Bunyan "able to shoulder a barrel of salt pork weighing 330 pounds and walk off without any effort"; Pennsylvanian W.W. Hale, who gave his men two days off, Saturday to wash clothes and Sunday for the sabbath, and earned a reputation for that simple act; Nathaniel Tibbets, a Maine logger who moved from St. Croix to Grand Rapids with his sons and the railroad; and all the Minneapolis lumbermen: Dorilus Morrison, Joel Bassett, Ankeny and Company, Eastmen Bovey and Company — these and others came to Grand Rapids to cut the pine in winter and ride the logs down the Father of Waters in the spring. The first building in Grand Rapids was a store built of white pine logs in the early seventies. When the Duluth and Winnipeg rails reached the community as the last decade of the nineteenth century began, the village that formed around the store incorporated. Iron discoveries were producing a boom at the time, and it wasn't until this boom developed that the first mill went into operation producing lath and shingles. The last log drive went down the Mississippi from the Itasca County region in 1918, and the mill closed. But unlike Hermansville, Grand Rapids continued to thrive and grow. There were many reasons. When the pine was gone, the numerous lakes nearby turned the area into resort country. The cutover land away from the lakes was used for dairy farming or reverted to woodlands where the broadleaf aspen and birch dominated occasional stands of spruce, red pine, and cedar. The broadleafs held the secret of survival for the new human community. They began to feed what would become one of the largest papermills built in the old dominion of the pines. The mill began operations sixteen years before the last log drive. At mid-century, it was producing 150 tons of paper per day. The trees that could live with the new man, that could supply the paper that would make Americans one of the world's most broadly literate people, that could supply the demand for cheaper materials to build houses for ever-increasing numbers of humankind, and that could grow fast enough to be cut every twenty years were not the white pine, *Pinus strobus*. The broadleaf aspen, cloning itself through its root system, spreading its cottony seeds in dry years, growing back to total dominance after each fire were, after all, probably the oldest living things in Minnesota. Aspen root systems had been waging their war with the pine for some time. Some of the current clones are growing on root systems over 30,000 years old. As is usual with living things, there is a time of waxing and a time of waning. As the ice retreated and human culture flourished, as the Europeans cleared their forests and turned west to the new land, as the pine fell in Maine, Michigan, Wisconsin, and Minnesota, the aspen came into its time, a mass tree to live with the new mass man, a corporate tree interlocked with other trees, a democratic tree sharing its roots with all of its kind. The lordly pine fell to make man free and secure in the new world. With the pine passed elk and cougar; the numbers of moose and wolf shrank drastically; men and deer, companions of the broadleafs, ruled the new communities of living things in what had been the pineries.

ALGER SMITH & CO. CAMP NO 6 SEC. 58 · 61 · 4.
COOK CO, MINN, 1916   PHOTO. BY ROLEFF

The cook and his "cookies" in a Cook, Minnesota kitchen and dining building in 1916. *Courtesy, Minnesota Historical Society. Photo: William Roleff — Two Harbors, Mn.*

Cook calling the logging crew to dinner. Each horn sounded slightly different and each cook had his own special call so that crews from different companies who were working together would recognize their camp's call. *Courtesy, Minnesota Historical Society.*

A "rack of pork" for hearty appetites. *Courtesy, Minnesota Historical Society. Photo: William Roleff, Two Harbors, Mn.*

The cook and his "cookies". Note the row of bread loaves, cookies and bisquits on the left.
Courtesy, Minnesota Historical Society. Photo: William Roleff, Two Harbors, Mn.

The cook house at the Bundy Lumber Company Camp #9 in Bundy, Wisconsin. *Courtesy, Oshkosh Public Museum.*

(Opposite page, top)
A pine load coming into the mill on a Sunday morning in 1892 from Camp #15 of the Wisconsin Land & Timber Company in Hermansville, Michigan. *Courtesy, Wisconsin Land & Timber Company.*

(Opposite page, bottom)
The lunch crew after returning from delivering lunch to the men in the field. *Courtesy, Wisconsin Land & Timber Company, Hermansville, Michigan.*

Sitting down to a meal in silence. Talking was forbidden during meals in most logging camps as it slowed up the men, the cooks and the cookies. *Courtesy, Minnesota Historical Society. Photo: William Roleff, Two Harbors, Mn.*

The logging camp foreman in the camp office. Most day-to-day decisions were made in this office as well as the preparation of paychecks, supply orders, hirings and firings. *Courtesy, State Historical Society of Wisconsin.*

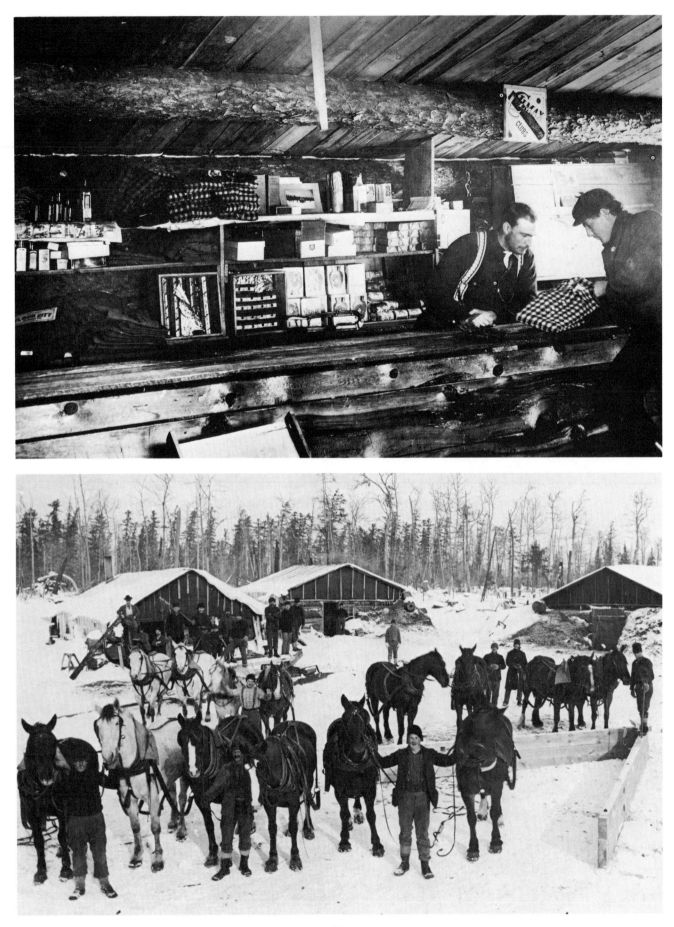

Boarding house for loggers and mill workers in Hermansville, Michigan. *Courtesy, Wisconsin Lane & Timber Company, Hermansville, Michigan.*

(Opposite page, top)
The company "van" or supply store. *Courtesy, State Historical Society of Wisconsin.*

(Opposite page, bottom)
Teamsters with their horses at the Schroeder Camp in Michigan in 1896. *Courtesy, Marquette County Historical Society.*

27

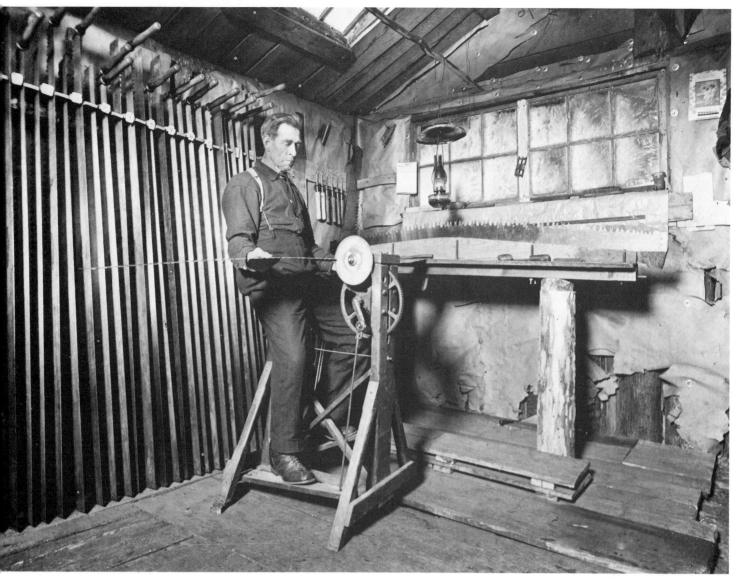

Saw filer at Kileen & Company's Hindall Camp #1 in 1914. Every logging camp had at least one man whose only job was to sharpen and set the teeth of the company saws. This was done both in the woods and in the "filing shack" in camp. *Courtesy, Minnesota Historical Society. Photo: William Roleff, Two Harbors, Mn.*

(Opposite page, top)
Part of the Rumley Crew of the Alger Company in Michigan. *Courtesy, Marquette County Historical Society.*

(Opposite page, bottom)
Wisconsin Land & Timber Company store in the 1920's. Loggers and their families could purchase goods here on credit against their yearly wages. *Courtesy, Wisconsin Land & Timber Company, Hermansville, Michigan.*

The problem of shoeing oxen was the main reason why they were gradually replaced by horses in the logging camps. The blacksmith could not pick up an ox's foot to put a shoe on it as he could with a horse. If an ox's foot is lifted off the ground, the ox will either lie or fall down. Consequently, elaborate racks such as this one were constructed which lifted the ox for shoeing. Shoeing the ox was further complicated because the animal required two shoes per foot; shoes which came off easily when the ox was hauling logs along ice roads. *Courtesy, State Historical Society of Wisconsin.*

(Opposite page, top)
Shoeing horses in a logging camp blacksmith shop in 1912. *Courtesy, Minnesota Historical Society. Photo: William Roleff, Two Harbors, Mn.*

(Opposite page, bottom)
The blacksmith shop in a logging camp. *Courtesy, Itasca County Historical Society.*

Minnesota logging camp company "van" or store. The Company van was the source of supply
for the loggers' daily needs such as snuff, tobacco, knives, shirts, pants, socks and liniment.
Courtesy, Minnesota Historical Society. Photo: William Roleff, Two Harbors, Mn.

(Opposite page, top)
Cook shanty at Lammers Brothers Pigeon Lake camp at Drummond, Wisconsin in 1893.
Courtesy, Minnesota Historical Society. Photo: John Runk.

(Opposite page, bottom)
Loggers in front of the camp office at Prairie River, Minnesota in 1910. *Courtesy, Itasca
County Historical Society.*

A mining company logging camp in Minnesota in 1912. Mining companies frequently formed logging companies in order to meet the mining companies' needs for mine timbers and rail ties. *Courtesy, Minnesota Historical Society. Photo: William Roleff, Two Harbors, Mn.*

Wilson Logging Company No. 1 at the north end of Island Lake in 1906. Approximately 35 million feet of logs were cut from this camp site. *Courtesy, Minnesota Historical Society.*

"Bull cook" sharpening an ax in the bunk house. Note that the sharpening wheel runs through a trough filled with water in order to keep it from filling with filings and to maintain a lower temperature during sharpening so that the ax will not lose its "temper" or hardness. *Courtesy, Iron Range Historical Society.*

Teamsters' sleeping quarters and part of the crew of an Oliver Iron Mining Company Camp during the winter of 1914. *Courtesy, Northeast Minnesota Historical Center.*

(Opposite page, top)
Sunday was laundry day in the logging camps. This photograph shows loggers on their day off at a camp in Barron County, Wisconsin in 1913. *Courtesy, State Historical Society of Wisconsin.*

(Opposite page, bottom)
A typical northeast Minnesota logging camp in the early 1900's. *Courtesy, Northeast Minnesota Historical Center.*

Sunday was not only laundry day in the camps but also haircut day as well. Men would cut each other's hair and occasionally, a traveling barber would visit the camp. Frequently, the barber would also perform necessary dental work such as pulling teeth. *Courtesy, Minnesota Historical Society. Photo: William Roleff, Two Harbors, Mn.*

(Opposite page, top)
Logging camp #29 between Bovey and Taconite, Minnesota, 1909. *Courtesy, Itasca County Historical Society.*

(Opposite page, bottom)
A crew of the Wisconsin Land & Timber Company, early 1900's. *Courtesy, Wisconsin Land & Timber Company, Hermansville, Michigan.*

A logging crew, March 9, 1906. *Courtesy, State Historical Society of Wisconsin.*

(Opposite page, top)
A logging camp operated by B. O. McGee near Rails Prairie, Minnesota in 1889. *Courtesy, Minnesota Historical Society.*

(Opposite page, bottom)
Lumberjacks of Jim Lane's logging camp taken in the winter of 1887. *Courtesy, Minnesota Historical Society. Photo: John Runk.*

41

Helvi Nivukoski in front of a lumber camp cook shack in Minnesota in 1903. She was a cook in a logging camp near Mt. Iron, Minnesota. *Courtesy, Minnesota Historical Society.*

(Opposite page, top)
The interior of a typical 1900's bunkhouse. Generally there was an older worker, called the "bull cook" who would be responsible for keeping the wood pile stocked and water in the watercans. Pot bellied stoves such as this one were very inefficient and many times had only two heat ranges — too hot or too cold! *Courtesy, Minnesota Historical Society. Photo: William Roleff, Two Harbors, Mn.*

(Opposite page, bottom)
Bunk house in a northern Minnesota logging camp in the early 1900's. Obviously, wet clothing was always a problem when working in the woods in the winter! *Courtesy, Northeast Minnesota Historical Center.*

A bunkhouse scene from a lumber camp. The bench the men are sitting on was called the "deacon's seat". *Courtesy, Minnesota Historical Society.*

(Opposite page, top)
Loggers on the "deacon bench" in a Minnesota logging camp bunkhouse, early 1900's. *Courtesy, Itasca County Historical Society.*

(Opposite page, bottom)
Interior of a logging camp bunkhouse around 1905. *Courtesy, Marquette County Historical Society.*

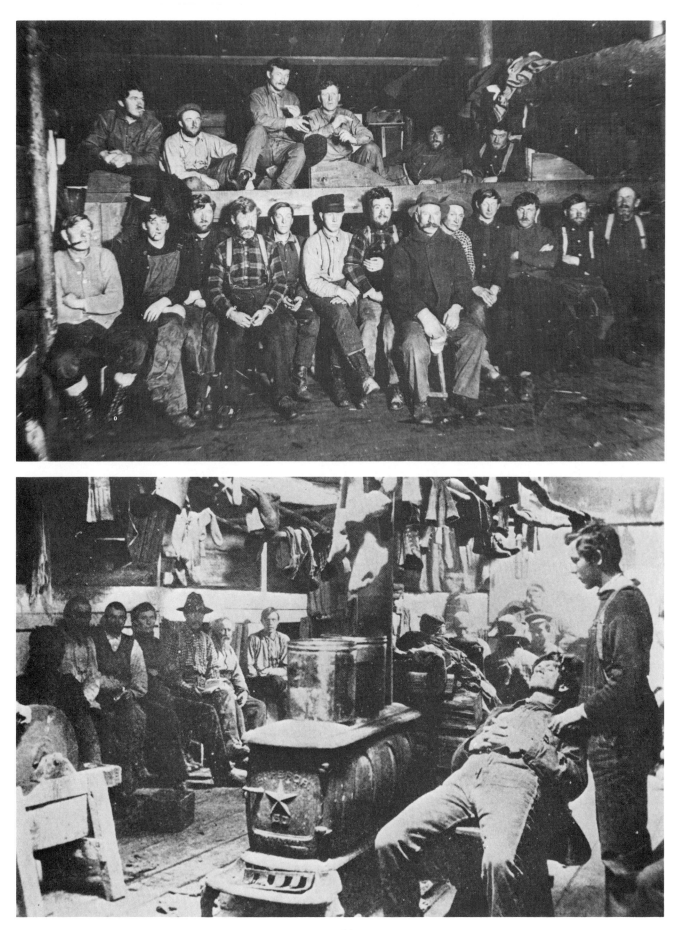

Logging camp bunkhouse in northern Minnesota in 1906. *Courtesy, The Nyman Collection.*

Many camps maintained a supply of "meat on the hoof". Pork was a staple in most camp meals.
Courtesy, State Historical Society of Wisconsin.

The cook and "cookies" lined up before the tables prior to a meal. Logging camp cooking and eating utensils were similar across Wisconsin, Michigan and Minnesota because supplies came from a small number of outlets and years of use had proven the utensils' utility and longevity. *Courtesy, State Historical Society of Wisconsin.*

CHAPTER THREE

The Army of Light:
The Shantyboys

*"For there are woods to people,
And there is a trail to make."*

THE FIRST agents of the broadleafs' new campaign were landlookers, or timber cruisers. Following the trails of the hunters and trappers, French and Indian, they climbed the tallest pines on the highest hills and spied the outposts, villages, and cities of the pine; noted the waterways leading to the enclaves; and claimed the pines for man. Like the voyageur who went before him, the timber cruiser began by entering the "edge of night," the dominion of the pines, to find its secrets and claim from it a livelihood. The cruisers walked the pineries from Maine to Minnesota, paddled up streams from the Penobscot to the Rainy, seeking first the best stands nearest water, then the best still standing in the cutovers, and finally, with the coming of ice roads and railroads, the far stands of the pine. Like all of America's early woodsmen, they were men of great skill and courage; they traveled the unmapped wilds by compass, made their own maps, set boundary markers for the timber they claimed. They pressed ever west and north into the heart of the domain of the pines where none save trappers, traders, and Indians had gone before. They traveled in crews of two or three, on snowshoes, afoot, or by canoe. They raced each other to the timber and back to the land offices. In the mid-fifties, a pair of cruisers named Daniel Ward and John Bailey made a difficult trek up the Tittabawassee and the Tobacco and overland to a region west of Otsego Lake in search of cork pines. There they spent three weeks mapping the best stands in the region. Then, fearing that a competitor would claim the timber they had found, the two men began an odyssey on land and water to Saginaw, Michigan, raced by rail and stage to Detroit to obtain the money necessary to pay for the claims, drove eighteen hours by buggy to Lansing, and finished by riding a stage to the land office in Ionia where they entered and paid for the claims. Their rivals walked into the same land office twenty-four hours later, too late to claim the green gold of the Otsego region.

The cruisers were the key to a successful lumbering operation. Carrying all they needed to sustain themselves for long weeks in the wild, the cruising teams moved over the newly opened treaty lands, found the lakes and streams of each region, gauged the number of board feet in each stand, and foresaw the problems involved in moving the bodies of the fallen giants to landings. They planned the campaign to fell the pines they had spied, laying out approaches, picking the giants to be brought low, describing the treasures to be found in each city and village of the pine. They returned with word of the wild and its treasures. "Seventy mills in seventy years couldn't exhaust the white pine I have seen on the Rum River," Daniel Stanchfield told the men who sent him landlooking. After listening to his account, the men proceeded to cut the Rum River pine to Lake Mille Lacs, from mouth to source.

Lyman Ayers was born in a pioneer cabin seven years before the first logs of the St. Croix Valley were milled. The cabin was in Crawford County, Michigan Territory, in what became Pine County, Minnesota, near what would become Pine City — saw town for the Kettle River pines. Ayers was a pioneer school teacher, a buffalo hunter, and a scout, carrying dispatches between Fort Snelling and Fort Gary north of what is now Winnipeg. He was also a voyageur fur trader in the Red River country. When he began cruising timber, Ayers invented a new system for estimating the board feet in the stands he cruised, sold his information first to jobbers, then to the Northern Pacific, and finally to Backus and Brooks of Minneapolis. He cruised at 74, and died at 87 in 1919. During a lifetime that had spanned the final stages of the battle between conifer and broadleaf, Ayers saw the new civilization rise out of the wood that fell. The first pine he cruised was clear cork pine that sold for twenty-five cents a thousand; the last was the scrub left in the cutovers — still white pine — that sold for fourteen dollars a thousand. A quiet, sober man who spoke French, Ojibway, and Dakota as well as English, Lyman Ayers wore moccasins until he served in the Civil War and loved the ways of the wild. He passed with the passing of the wild, fell with the last of the pines.

The first logging crews in the pineries of the Midwest followed where their scouts led, up the waterways into the pines. For the most part, the crews were led by men from Maine and consisted of two choppers, two or three swampers, two sled tenders, two sawyers, one teamster with six to eight oxen, and one cook. Such a team was expected to cut a million board feet of logs during a winter. The choppers were the aristocrats of the early crews, axmen whose skill in felling the trees in precisely the right way made the work of everyone else easier. When they "fleshed their axes" in a new stand of white pine, the final battle between broadleaf and pine was joined. They saw themselves as soldiers of civilization, as conquerors wielding their axes in conquest. Listen to the "Song of the Western Pioneer," printed in the *Stillwater Messenger* in June of 1867.

> Hurray for the axe, the brave sharp axe,
> Hurrah for its notes that ring,
> Through the valley wide, up the mountain side,
> When it sweeps like a falcons wing.
> And down crashes the pine, with its lordly crest,
> For the axe hath cleaved through its knotted breast.
> Let others sing of the sword and flash
> Of a forest of dancing spears;
> But their path is red with the blood of the dead,
> Whilst behind them a sea of tears.
> And the maiden shall wait for her lover in vain,
> For he sleeps where the moon beams glance cold on
>   the stain.
> Not such thy triumph, my brave sharp axe,
> On your blade are no stains of sin,
> With a sweep and a blow, you strike your foe
> And up from his grave doth spring
> The yellow grain, the broad leaved corn,
> And my children bless you at early morn.

The swampers wielded the ax as well, trimming the appendages of the lordly pine, clearing brush in trails that led from each fallen pine to a landing or loading deck. The barkers stripped the bark from what would become the underside of the tree to allow it to slide more easily. The sled tenders, or chainers, worked with the teamster moving the fallen tree onto the go-devil, a wishbone-shaped device with a crossbar made from the crotch of a hardwood tree, chained the log in place, and made way for the teamster to drag the long trunk through brush and snow along the swamper's skidding trails to the landing. There the sawyers cut the trunk into sixteen-foot lengths. Finally, these sticks were banked so that they could be rolled into lake or stream when high water made it possible to drive the logs to mills and markets.

These early logging crews lived in shanties, or "state-of-Maine" camps. The shanties were log sheds built in late fall to accommodate the team close to the pine they came to conquer. The earliest shanties, low walled and steep roofed, housed twenty to twenty-five shantyboys, foot soldiers in the struggle between broadleaf and pine. The shanty was dark and sometimes low walled enough so that the jacks had to bend to enter. In the center was an open fire under a hole in the roof. Here bread baked, clothing dried, the chill was driven from hand and foot, and the night was held at bay. Once the year's campaign had begun, the fire, or "caboose," as the shantyboys called it, often burned continuously, fed by the scraps of pine, maple, birch, and aspen that the battle between the species produced. Along one side of the shanty were balsam-bough beds, arranged by each man to his specifications, and on each pile of boughs, head to the wall, feet to the fire, the crewmen rested their heads on their "turkeys," the simple bags that contained all a man carried with him to the woods. Across from the sleeping campaigners and spread along the wall of the shanty were a kitchen, a washing area, and a toolroom, with grindstones, sinks, and water barrels. The cook prepared meals for the crew at the open fire, moving kettles over the fire using a wooden crane. He also prepared beans — a shantyboy staple — by baking them in a bean hole, a four-foot-deep excavation in which a covered steel kettle resting on and surrounded by coals cooked beans overnight while cook and all slept. Bread, salt pork, and blackstrap molasses were the staples for the shantyboys. They supplemented this simple fare as they could with venison, fish, and fowl. Initially, tea, the preferred beverage of the Maine lumbermen, was the only beverage served in the shanty, but as the crews of the Lake States pineries began to hear the sounds of Norwegian, Swedish, and Finnish, coffee was added.

The shantyboys work from first light to last. Up two hours before daybreak, the teamster feeds and hitches his oxen, the cook feeds teamsters, swampers, choppers, sawyers, tenders; all save the cook and, in larger camps, his helper follow the foreman into the woods before the break of day. As first light filters down to the rusty floor of the pinery, the foreman, wielding his "brave sharp axe" undercuts the day's first pine to lay it on the skidding trail, and the choppers flesh their ringing axes in the opposite side of the same tree. As the foreman turns his ax to other pines, for the first time the cry of "Timber-r-r!" And then the slow, silent start, the crack followed by another short silence, the sound of wind in treetops, the earth-shaking explosion, and clouds of flying snow. The heady satisfaction all small things know in seeing great things fall. Next, the swampers step in, filling the air with the sound of axes, and the oxen begin to move into place with some rattling of chains, some creaking of harness. The day has begun, the battle is rejoined, the mighty have fallen.

That night in camp, the meal done, sitting on a split log running the length of the shanty (the "deacon's bench"), wearing old cutoff boots or stags, their wet socks and underwear hanging to dry, the shantyboys will trade some stories, perhaps sing a song or two, smoke a pipe, but before too long each will fall to his bed of boughs; for the morrow will begin two hours before dawn, and bone and muscle will drive cold steel until night falls. This is the way it will be for six days out of seven. On the Sabbath, there is washing, card playing, mending, and cutting new boughs of balsam for beds. The world is being remade with singing steel, with saw and ax, and on the seventh day, the shantyboys rest with satisfaction.

When it came time for the log drive, the second battalion — the riverhogs — took charge. Using pike and peavey or cant dog, they broke the banked logs loose into streams and rivers and rode the bounding logs downstream, through rapids, past falls in flumes to the mill. Here there was no rest on any day. From April to September, whenever and wherever the water would float white pine, the rivermen danced their dance, leaping from log to log, pushing and poling, leaping into waist-deep water, thrusting floating ice aside to roll logs off sand bars, working wet through in snow and sleet. They moved on the logs, up and down the banks, carrying an oilcloth nose bag on their backs, with biscuits, ham, and hardboiled eggs to be eaten when the logs permitted. Behind the logs floated the wanigans, sheds on shallow draft barges where cooking and sleeping were done. Sometimes there were camps along the drive route, and the riverhog walked upstream to meet the logs or down to catch them. But at other times there was no sleeping and no eating. The river of white-pine battering rams had to move through churning rapids, pounding against the ancient rocks of the waterway, temporarily catching and piling, then breaking loose as the skillful twisting, pushing, spinning with pike poles, peaveys, and cant hooks loosened the knot of wood. A sound like an explosion, and on the wood flowed, bank to bank, mile after mile covered with logs cut by crew after crew. The cities were growing; their needs were profound; the cities paid coin of the realm. So the riverhogs rode the roaring logs out of the wild into the mills. The moment the skidding trails turned to mud, the loggers dropped saw and ax, changed from rubber boots to corks, and picked up pike and peavey. When they broke the rollways at the landings, the logs piled through the winter roared down into the water. There was danger to life and limb from that moment on. Arms and legs were

broken with the rollways, and occasionally, a wild log struck down a swamper before he could become a white-water birler. Once the logs were in the water, the rapids and log jams killed riverhogs each year. In a river of grinding logs whose muttering could be heard for miles, those who fell found no way to swim. Death rode the logs with the riverhogs and claimed them at will. The rivermen changed their uniforms to ride with death. Not only did they put on the spiked corks which scarred the saloon floors of hundreds of mill towns, but they shed their heavy mackinaws of wool and switched from woolen pants to stagged overalls with the legs cut off at boot top.

The men who survived the drives year after year were of a piece. They were all, to use their own term, "catty." They could move or stand on the bucking logs, leap from log to log, and balance on logs racing down a flume at a forty-five-degree angle. When the jams came, with logs piling, twisting, and knotting into a seemingly impossible tangle, and the water built pressure behind the jam, flooding the banks and occasionally a riverside town, the rivermen danced with death. They knew what must be done: find the king log, plant the cant dog, twist, and then as the rumbling started, leap and run on the falling, twisting, bucking river of white pine; run for the edge of the thundering woodfall; and in mad and magic moments, dicing with death, making it, lying on the bank, laughing, being pounded as he rises, the French twang, the Scots burr, the Irish brogue, the slow Scandinavian lilts, all singing a hymn to courage, manhood, victory in the battle with the giants. And if, instead, a sudden wild twist, a flip of a ton of logs, or a flight above the rolling, tumbling, roaring, thundering wood, a scream unheard by any save the thrashing giants, and a short burst of pain exploding in the brain like a flash of light, still on the tongues of the survivors, in all the accents of the woods, a hymn, a dirge about courage, manhood, and defeat.

At the end of the drive, the survivors "blew it in." It is in the tales of these moments of whooping and whoring, of drinking and dancing, of fighting and feeding that the legends of the jacks were born. Men who dice daily with death and win are the same the world over. These soldiers in the broadleaf brigade were no different. From November to September, they worked felling, dragging, rolling, and riding the lords of the wild, and they had won again; they'd brought home the wood; they were taming the wild; they were letting daylight into the primal dark; they were making way for "the yellow grain, the broadleaf corn"; they were building the nation. They'd worked for a dollar a day or less in the woods, for two to five dollars for a day and night on the killing water, and what they had earned was paid at exactly the moment the logs reached the mill. What they paid out for snoose, boots, and undershirts at the camp store was deducted; but for a moment they had money. In the barrooms they bought drinks for the other survivors and paid for the softness and femininity they had dreamed of in the dark shanty, blowing it all in, celebrating their annual victory over death and the darkness of the edge of night in a rite as ancient as the Dionysian orgies of Crete and Greece 4,000 years earlier. The workers of the field had harvested their crop; the soldiers of civilization had finished the campaign; the wood was in the mill; the time for celebration was at hand. As logging moved from Maine to the Lake States and particularly as it moved to the Mississippi Valley, there would be more steps between woods and mill and a whole new battalion of heroes. As technology changed logging, the romance and the dying would pass. But in the beginning it was muscle and bone against wood and water, and the victory over the wild was celebrated in ways as old as civilization.

In the valley of the Mississippi, along the Wisconsin, the Black, the Chippewa, the St. Croix, at St. Anthony Falls and in St. Paul there were mills, but the chief market for much of the lumber sawed at these mills was downriver at Davenport, Muscatine, Quincy, or St. Louis. As the first milling on the Upper Mississippi took place, the first rafting began. A lumber raft arrived at St. Louis from Portage, Wisconsin, in 1839. Twenty years later, 3,000 men were engaged in lumbering on the Wisconsin River, and all the lumber they cut was floated down through the upper rapids, fourteen miles of churning Mississippi waters, dropping twenty-two feet, stretching from LeClaire, Iowa, to Rock Island, the bare rock splitting the stream, and when wind and water were wrong, destroying the rafts, on to the Des Moines and the lower rapids, running from the junction of the Des Moines and the Mississippi, from Montrose to Keokuk. In the twelve miles between Muscatine and Keokuk, the river dropped twenty-four feet. Just as the riverhogs had ridden their logs down the broiling headwaters of the Mississippi flowage, the raftmen rode rafts of cut lumber down the Father of Waters. Some of them were the same axmen and swampers who had felled the pines and ridden the logs on spring freshets to the mill. They spent their summers manning the sweeps, tightening or loosening the lines, riding the last of the rapids past Keokuk, and drifting at last into St. Louis, with its floating dance halls, gaslights, and painted women. They hit Muscatine, Quincy, or St. Louis the same way they'd hit Stillwater, but downriver, in what was becoming farm country and town and city, somehow the raftmen seemed wilder than the riverhogs. Perhaps the closer to the edge of night one was, the easier it was to understand the soldiers of the army of light.

The very center of early rafting was the raft pilot, a man capable of reading the ever-changing sandbars of the upper river, of sensing the interplay of wind and current, of feeling the shifting of his immense raft, of telling his crew to loosen lines to bend the raft back on itself in following the twisting river. The pilot knew every bend of the river, every line of hills, each new bluff. He knew what draft of water at what stages of the river; his pulse beat with the pulse of the continent. And such men knew their worth; risking thousands of dollars, the millowners and yardmen of Iowa, Illinois, and Missouri paid Dave Philomalee, Bill Skinner, Bill Simons, Sandy McPhail, and Wild Penny Joe Blow three to five hundred a month to float lumber and logs to them. When high water on the St. Croix in the summer of 1843 caused the St. Croix boom to break and a whole season's logs scattered downriver, one John B. Page gathered logs, rafted them, and rode the high water to St. Louis selling to Mr. Thomas West. After that, logs too were rafted downriver. For the next seventy years, white pine logs and lumber would be rafted to mills from Winona to St. Louis. In the beginning, as with all white pine lumbering, it was done by hand; the raft pilot standing in the middle, "attired in French calf boots, black cashmere trousers, finely knitted red flannel shirt, a large black silk necktie tied in a square knot with flowing ends, and a soft, wide brimmed black or white hat . . . master of all he surveyed," barked his orders — "Left behind, right in front" — and a crew of twenty to thirty-five manned the massive sweeps and played out or snugged down lines. If the water was high, six brails, or units bound together with check works, crosslines, A lines, cornerlines, fifteen hundred feet by three hundred, an island of pine, twisted through the bends. A skilled pilot, by loosing lines, could bend the raft into "C" or "S" shapes. The crew and the pilots worked as long as the raft traveled, night and day. They ate and slept in shifts, in the cook shed at the center of the raft and in the individual shanties that dotted the back of the raft. And there was always danger, always uncertainty, often disaster. They wrote to the log or lumber owners and told their tales.

"With regard to two rafts of white pine logs belonging to Franklin Steele Esq. and by him placed in charge of Herrall & Jackson for safe running to St. Louis or a market. That said Herrall & Jackson were pilots — ordered to send to St. Paul 4 men to couple up a quantity of Pine Logs in St. Pauls. To form 2 rafts to consist of six strings each. Done October 8, 1850. Herrall came to Pigs Eye (the St. Paul landing) on October 10, 1850. Herrall left with 2 strings from Pigs Eye. On way down he picked up 4 other strings left by Mr. Steeles rafting crew at a convenient point and intended for a descending raft. Franklin no. 2 (a steamer) took them thro Lake Pepin — Bill sent to Mr. Steel for that. After leaving Lake Pepin raft was formed in three divisions and after considerable difficulty because of low water we finally arrived at Holmes, a trading post.

Then formed into two rafts. Herrall had charge of one and one Wm Ganly of other. Below Holmes Herrall struck a bow head and carried away about 200 logs. At Prairie LaCrosse Herrall stuck his raft on a sandbar. Ganly tried to push Herrall off but thus Ganly injured his raft and spent 3 days refitting. Then Herralls raft went to pieces. Herrall then decided to leave logs there until spring. Herrall was so disgusted that he said "God Damn the Logs and God damn Steel that he had done with the logs for ever, and for all time. They might go to Hell."

And so the islands of pine made their way from Rum River hillside to the prairies of Oklahoma. And the army of light, the vanguard of civilization, drove the edge of night further north and west. The warriors rode the backs of the fallen titans down the roaring St. Croix, Black, Rum, through the mills at Stillwater, LaCrosse, St. Anthony, or past them, on through Lake Pepin, sailing the lake with blankets tied to shanty boards, or cordelling — walking the shore and pulling the raft. They pulled twenty-seven miles, then on past Winona, on to LeClaire and the Rock Island Rapids, Montrose, and the Lower Rapids, Muscatine, Keokuk, and St. Louis. Like the legions of Rome, they brought the conquered back to serve civilization, singing as they went — singing of the dark winter woodlands, the falling giants, singing of death and the muddy brown boiling waters of the drive, singing of sun and rain, wind and water, and life on the river.

There were jobs to be done, however, of which no one sang. The total numbers of crews in the woods in all parts of the pineries grew at an incredible rate, and as the logs drifted to the mills, the timber of one cutting crew mingled with that of another. Angry exchanges between log owners abounded, and chaos ruled. So the boom companies were born, as were log marks, branding axes, and eventually, corporations. By running a line of floating logs chained together across the channel of major logging rivers, boom operators were able to stop logs, swing them out of the main channel into calm water, examine the log marks, and sort each owner's logs into rafts which could then be floated to mills stretching from Marine to St. Louis. The boomers scaled the logs cut by independent jobbers to determine how many board feet each contained so that millowners could pay the independent timbermen who had felled the trees and owned the logs. The booms were generally cooperative efforts in which several millowners invested capital to ensure themselves of logs to cut and to avoid the problems of confused ownership. Substantial numbers of men, including some of the lumbering crews back from the woods, worked with pike and peavey to move and sort the logs. Frequently, the newly arrived immigrants, looking for work to buy their seed, spent time working at the booms. The dangers of romance of woods,

river, and raft were lacking, but the booms were at the heart of the emerging lumber industry, sending the flow of wood to the mills. In fact, as the booms developed it became apparent that skillful entrepreneurs could control the supply of logs to their competitors, and twenty years of legislative and legal battles about the rights and responsibilities of boom operators began as the Beef Slough boom began its operations. From those battles, Fredric Weyerhaeuser and the Mississippi Valley Lumberman's Association would emerge as the first great lumbering corporation. As surely as the opening chapters of white pine logging are the story of the soldiers of fortune who cut and rode the pine, it is also the story of the captains of industry, who came to direct the continuing battle of broadleafs with conifers in the far reaches of the Pacific Northwest.

And what of the makers of wood — the sawyers and millwrights who turned logs to lumber? Here is a story that perhaps should be sung. Nowhere did the technology of the lumber industry develop more rapidly than in the mills. When white pine logging and lumbering began on the coast of Maine in the seventeenth century, the basic mode of cutting boards was the two-man whipsaw or pit saw. One sawyer stood above the log on a platform, a second stood in a pit below the log. They pushed and pulled the saw between them. This method dated back to the pharaohs of Egypt. But change was afoot, and as the white pine era dawned, a gate or sash saw — a blade contained in a wooden frame — had been invented; and if the frame was heavy enough and if water power was available, the saw could be operated at high speed with the weight of the sash on the saw providing the cutting power on the downstroke. With slight refinements, steam power could be applied and a number of gate saws could be positioned side by side. And so the gang saw was born. Mill output moved from thousands of board feet per year to millions. Simultaneously, a totally different sawing technique was being developed, and by the time logging was established in the Lake States, circular saws, invented in England during the American revolution, joined the industrial revolution and revolved through billions of feet of white pine. The first American circular saw was produced as the War of 1812 ended, and the mills of Maine and New York cut white pine with them before moving west to the Lake States.

Who were the Lake States sawyers? At first they were specialists brought from Maine by ads and by their desire to find a place where they might make their own fortunes. They became owners and lumbermen rather than sawyers. After them came a new generation of sawyers from Germany. They began as millhands stacking and sorting, learned to operate the saws, and moved on to build and operate their own mills. Fredric Weyerhaeuser was one such immigrant. He formed his syndicate to buy the Beef Slough boom to ensure that he would have logs and bought his towboats to move his rafts of logs more swiftly to the mill he had built at Rock Island on land that cost him $500. His syndicate bought the spruce of the Northwest to ensure a log supply when the last of the pine passed. And when the pine did pass, he sold tamarack to the railroads for ties, cedar to the farmers and ranchers for their posts, and poles to the telephone and telegraph companies. He was the living embodiment of the immigrant's dream of what America could be. As the century turned, the German millhand became the lumber baron, a legend in his own time.

These, then, were the battalions of the army of light, the men who felled the giants as the final campaign of the broadleafs was mounted in Maine, New York, Pennsylvania, Michigan, Wisconsin, and Minnesota. They came from Canada, New Brunswick, Quebec, and Ontario, speaking French and English with a Scots burr or an Irish brogue. They moved from Maine west, and their ranks were swelled by Germans in Wisconsin, by Swedes and Norwegians in central and northwestern Minnesota, and by Finns as the Duluth district and north shore holdouts fell. And where there had been the edge of night, there was light.

A Minnesota tie-maker. The ax that a tie-maker used was flat on one side to allow him to hew logs square for use as railroad ties. *Courtesy, Itasca County Historical Society.*

The Kidder Land Looking party, 1862. From right to left, Captain Bridges, Mr. Banfield, Walter Kidder, Fred Johnson, and Alfred Kidder, Sr. The boy is unidentified. As timber resources were exhausted, parties such as this one would travel into new areas to "cruise" for timber and river routes. *Courtesy, Marquette County Historical Society.*

(Opposite page, top)
Two undercutters at work in the pineries of Minnesota. To make the tree fall in the exact place desired, the undercutters notched the tree on a certain side. This was done before the sawyers started to saw the tree down. *Courtesy, Minnesota Historical Society. Photo: John Runk.*

(Opposite page, bottom)
Sawyers in Michigan in the 1890's. *Courtesy, U.S. Library of Congress.*

Logging by the Algoma Company, Black River, Michigan in the 1880's. *Courtesy, Marquette County Historical Society*.

(Opposite page, top)
Sawing white pine in Wisconsin, around 1913. *Courtesy, State Historical Society of Wisconsin*.

(Opposite page, bottom)
Loggers with oxen and white pine saw bolts in the Minnesota woods, circa 1890. *Courtesy, NE Minnesota Historical Center*.

Mr. Ferguson, filing saws at the cutting site in −20 degrees weather in 1915. *Courtesy, Minnesota Historical Society.*

Springtime at the Morse and Tradewell lumber camp in 1912. Iver Johnson, the camp comedian is standing on his head. *Courtesy, Oshkosh Public Museum.*

gin white pine in Wisconsin. *Courtesy, State Historical Society of Wisconsin.*

A logger eating lunch in the field at −15 degrees in Winton, Minnesota. *Courtesy, Iron Range Historical Society.*

Bringing lunch to loggers in the field at the Fortier Logging Camp, Winton, Minnesota. *Courtesy, Iron Range Historical Society.*

Eating lunch in the field at the Fortier Logging Camp, Winton, Minnesota. *Courtesy, Iron Range Historical Society.*

Big Wheels at Logging Camp
1912

Logs were slung from the axle of "big wheels" during attempts to continue logging into the spring and summer months in Michigan. Generally unsuccessful, big wheels worked only in relatively flat, dry, inland forests. *Courtesy, Marquette County Historical Society.*

(Opposite page, top)
Getting out tamarack or spruce wanigan knees was quite a business in the early days of the woods. The knees were the trunk of the tree together with its large root which grew at a right angle to the trunk. It made a strong, tough, durable framework for the hull of a heavy boat. This picture was taken at Willow River, Minnesota in 1902. *Courtesy, Minnesota Historical Society.*

(Opposite page, bottom)
Using "big wheels" to skid logs from the site in Michigan in 1890. *Courtesy, U.S. Library of Congress.*

Loading logs onto rail cars using a steam engine instead of horses. *Courtesy, Oshkosh Public Museum.*

(Opposite page, top)
Filling water tanks for icing roads. These water sleighs would be filled at nearby lakes. Stoves were built into the sleds in order to keep the water from freezing. Once filled, the sleds were pulled over the logging roads and water was released into the ruts where it froze thereby making it easier for horses to pull large loads of logs to the rail siding or river bank. *Courtesy, Minnesota Historical Society.*

(Opposite page, bottom)
Filling the road icing sleigh at Fall Lake in Ely, Minnesota. *Courtesy, Iron Range Historical Society.*

Logging camp foreman holding a "peavey", a tool which assists the logger in rolling logs from one location to another. *Courtesy, Itasca County Historical Society.*

(Opposite page, top)
Side loading logs in Michigan around 1890. Probably about 90 percent of all logs were loaded onto sleighs by what was known as the "cross haul" method. In this method, a long chain was drawn over the load and under the center of the log and back to a team of horses for power. The other end of the chain was made fast and the log was rolled up a pair of skids onto the sleigh. *Courtesy, Marquette County Historical Society.*

(Opposite page, bottom)
A lumber camp crew with a "donkey engine" in the field in 1895. The donkey engines were portable steam engines which were used to assist horses in winching logs through the woods and in loading logs onto sleighs and railcars. *Courtesy, Minnesota Historical Society.*

69

Loading logs with a steam winch and boom in 1912. *Courtesy, Minnesota Historical Society.*
Photo: *William Roleff, Two Harbors, Mn.*

(Opposite page, top)
Loading full length white pine logs onto small rail cars in Black River, Michigan in 1884.
Courtesy, Marquette County Historical Society.

(Opposite page, bottom)
Side loading with horses in Minnesota. *Courtesy, Itasca County Historical Society.*

One of the largest loads ever loaded and hauled on a sleigh was loaded near Ewen, Michigan on Sunday, February 26, 1893. The load was composed of fifty logs of white pine and scaled 36,055 feet. Each tier excepting the top log was securely bound by a one half inch steel test chain. There were 850 feet of this chain which weighed 2,000 pounds. The load measured 30 feet 3 inches high by 18 feet long and weighed 40 tons. The load was hauled fifty rods by a team weighing 3,500 pounds. It was shipped to Chicago where it was a part of the Michigan exhibit at the World's Fair. Nine railway cars were required to transport this "World's Fair Load". *Courtesy, Minnesota Historical Society.*

(Opposite page, top)
Sanding hill in the Dead River District, 1901. Road maintenance men or "road monkeys" kept sand or straw in the downhill ruts of the logging roads in order to keep the loads of logs from catching up with the horses. Road monkeys also removed manure from the roads and repaired parts of the ice that had been chipped by the sharp calks of the horse. *Courtesy, Marquette County Historical Society.*

(Opposite page, bottom)
An unusually large load of logs which illustrates the skill of the "top-loader" or person who placed each log on the load. *Courtesy, State Historical Society of Wisconsin.*

A 12,800 board feet load of logs coming into Antigo, Wisconsin in 1907. *Courtesy, Oshkosh Public Museum.*

(Opposite page, top)
At first loggers relied upon oxen to haul logs to the river banks and loading sites. Because of the shoeing problems associated with oxen, however, they gradually shifted to the use of horses. *Courtesy, State Historical Society of Wisconsin.*

(Opposite page, bottom)
A prize load of logs at the Taft Camp in Minnesota in 1902. Note that each log is marked with its estimated amount of board feet. *Courtesy, Itasca County Historical Society.*

A fine load of logs photographed at Brackett's Camp division of the Anne River Logging
Company on the Anne River, Wisconsin in 1892. This load of logs scaled at 27,160 feet.
Courtesy, Minnesota Historical Society. Photo: John Runk.

(Opposite page, top)
A logging sled on the way to the landing on the St. Croix River in 1892. Log hauling was a work
that required the very highest of skill. Only the best of the log haulers could bring a heavy load
down the logging road to the landing. The St. Croix River developed perhaps the greatest log
haulers in the world. Logs were hauled to the St. Croix waters from a distance of twenty miles.
Courtesy, Minnesota Historical Society.

(Opposite page, bottom)
The crew of the Dead River Mill Company Camp #2 in 1901. *Courtesy, Marquette County
Historical Society.*

CHAPTER FOUR

The Way of the Pine: The Lumberjacks

As THE LAST decade of the nineteenth century began, white pine lumbering had become a way of life and a legend. The horse had replaced the ox as the chief dray animal, and the go-devil had been joined by the bobsled. Ice roads had replaced the old skidways, and thousands of men felled billions of board feet of logs annually using the crosscut saw instead of the ax. Only in undercutting and limbing did axes still ring. The shantyboys of Maine were now the lumberjacks of the Lake States, and their camps had become wilderness villages. There were new jobs, new top dogs among the jacks. The sawyers working in teams toppled the trees at new prodigious rates. Swampers still cut brush to build roads, banking grounds, landings, and skidding paths to the roads; but a whole new breed, road monkeys, worked continuously to maintain the iced sleigh roads. The hayman-on-the-hill dumped hay and dirt on the ruts gouged in the ice by a rut cutter to provide braking and prevent sleighs from overrunning horses. Top loaders did a new dance with mayhem, building sleigh loads, handling "big blues" with a "St. Croix" or a "Saginaw" twist of the cant hook. And there were scalers, inkslingers, landing men, cookees, bull cooks, deckers, rigging gangs, chainers, and teamsters, all doing specialized jobs. To feed the hungry maws of thousands of mills, white pine logging was growing more complex, more organized. The army of light began as the home guard, the militia; it was ending as organized as the legions of Rome or the army of the Republic.

Nowhere was the change more obvious than in the lumber camps. The one-room shanty had become a complex — a barracks for a hundred or more, with windows or skylights, a separate mess hall, stables, a shed for hay, a camp office and store, blacksmith shops, root houses, saw filers, shacks. Camp life was still full of long days of work, but the life of the lumberjack differed vastly from that of the shantyboy. The bunkhouse, home for the jack from November to April, was arranged with bunks instead of piles of boughs. The bunks, built along the wall, were filled first with hay and later with straw ticks. Built of cedar where possible to cut down on lice infestation, they might run as high as three tiers. If the jack climbed in from the end, his bed was a "muzzle-loader," from the side a "breech-loader." Each man used two blankets — one on the straw, one to cover his body. He still slept with his head on his turkey or tussock. A stove now stood in the center of the shed, but no cooking was done in the bunkhouse. A water barrel, a wash sink, and the deacon's bench completed the furnishings. A single, small kerosene lamp provided light until 9:00 when "lights out" sent the jacks to dreams of falling pine, river drives, and "blowing it in" at Saginaw, LaCrosse, or Duluth. High near the roof, wires were strung to hang the three to four pairs of wet woolen socks and mittens each man wore. Each man had his own wire space, and hanging out in someone else's space, overlooked once, would result in fried socks on subsequent occasions. The bull cook maintained the bunkhouse, supplying wood and water, washing the roller towel, cleaning the lamp chimney, replenishing kerosene and wicks, sweeping floors, blowing out the lights at 9:00. He rose before the men to build fires in the bunkhouse and the camp office.

At 4:00 in the morning, the cookee, the cook's helper, blew a five-foot tin horn. The sound could be heard for miles. The shanty boss called "Daylight in the swamp. R-r-roll out." And up they came from, as one lumber camp poet put it, "the land of dreams to the land of pork and beans." The camp kitchen was the cook's domain, and the cook and the cookee worked at the immense woodburning camp stove that had replaced the bean hole and caboose of the shanties. The cookhouse also contained long tables and benches where the men ate their meals. There were generally work tables, a sink, water barrels, camp kettles, bread pans, and tin dishes in abundance. A large griddle could be put in place to cover the top of the typical eight-lid range. Flapjacks for an army of hungry jacks leaving to meet the light of day couldn't be prepared with less. At midday, the cook sent the bull cook and cookee out in the "junk wagon" and fed the crews hot tea, beans, and bread around an open fire. "Flaggins," as the woods dinner was called, was often a frosty affair; food froze to plates and tea turned to ice if not downed quickly. When the crew returned at night as the moon, or "jobber's sun" rose, they found kitchen tables set and ready. The meal was eaten in silence. And the hungry jacks packed away salt pork, salted beef, or both, beans, potatoes, bread, tea or coffee, applesauce, rice pudding, cookies, doughnuts, and black molasses cake. Good cooking was one of the few real demands the lumbermen made. Crews "walked the cook" by going on strike, and bad cooks were replaced immediately to avoid losing a day of work from every man in the camp.

The camp office was a small structure providing sleeping space for the foreman, the scaler, and the camp clerk. In the office was another form of the wanigan. The term referred not only to the cooking and sleeping barges or the wagons that followed logging drives, but to the camp store. The jacks bought supplies ranging from mackinaws and rubber boots to tobacco and liniment. The camp clerk ran the store and kept records of the crew's work, wages, and purchases and maintained the log count and supplies and equipment inventories. The presence of the clerk in a camp full of axmen, sawyers, and teamsters is perhaps the clearest indication of the new style of the camps. Supplying large crews with everything from ax handles and horseshoe nails to snoose was not something that could be done in a single outfitting operation. Teamsters made regular runs between supply centers and the camps, and the clerk kept track of it all. Similarly, the scaler was a representative of the businesslike nature of the white pine camps of post–Civil War lumbering. His task was to estimate the number of board feet the logs would yield. As the problems of log supply multiplied and the demand increased, the millowners couldn't wait until the drive was over to scale their logs. The camps of the period were built and supplied by the millowners. Few of the independents were still cutting logs. Orders for lumber were coming from east and west. The scaler estimated the yield at the camp, the clerk sent his reports, the milling was planned, and the wood sold before a single log had rolled into a stream.

In stable, blacksmith shop, and saw shed it seemed at times that the work never stopped. The animals and equipment necessary to keep the trees falling and the logs moving had to be ready when the men were, and after all else was done for the day, teamsters fed and curried their animals, filers sharpened saws, blacksmiths replaced shoes and mended chains and tools. The team-

sters rose two hours before the rest of the crew to eat, feed and curry the horses, and harness the teams for work. All day they drove loads of 15,000 to 20,000 feet of logs on ice roads, down hay hills, to the banking yard, or snaked the newly bucked logs to landings on the ice road. Mistakes cost load, life, and limb. The men and horses returned in darkness, and the teamster turned first to caring for his animals. Hours after his comrades, he sat down to eat. First to rise, last to sleep. Not even time for a pipe on the deacon's bench or a stop at the wanigan.

So it was six days and nights in camp, but on the seventh day — break out the fiddles, mouth organs, mouth harps, accordions. Jig and reel. Play the ladies or the men. Dance and sing. Play at "hot bottom," striking the doubled-over tenderfoot with hands like a plank of pine; have him guess who and strike him again because he's always wrong. Laugh until the tears run. Shuffle the brogue and belt the fool who's "it" with the shoe he seeks, right across his cheeks. And laugh and laugh. Break out the cards — "fifteen two" and "I'll see you." Checkers and chanteys. O sing and laugh, for tomorrow's a day for "boiling up" and laying down. And what stories, what tales — about the toughest, the tallest, the meanest, the orneriest, the drinkingest, drunkest, hungriest, longest lasting, funniest, scariest of them all. Lumberjacks each and everyone; heroes of the tall tale, like all the other frontier men — cowboys, hunters, trappers, and mountain men — all the men who loved the edge of night, loved to lie about themselves and each other, to laugh at the credulous tenderfeet, to laugh at the pain in their backs, to flex the muscle in their arm, to laugh at the hours of work, to laugh at death or the weakness of old age, to brag past the fear and the loneliness, to choose life and laughter over tears and madness. Yes it was rough, yes it was at times meanspirited, yes there were moments of brutality; but there was also comradery, simple joy, imagination, and love — the love all soldiers know for comrades at arms.

Of what did they sing? Of what they did and what it meant.

A lumberjack's life is a wearisome one
Although some day it's free from care
It's the swinging an ax from morning to night
In forests wild and drear

Or sleeping in the bunkhouse dreary
While the winter winds do blow
But as soon as the morning star does appear
To the wild woods we must go

* * *

The rapids were raging
The waters were so high
Says the foreman to Swan Swanson
"This jam we'll have to try."

Swan Swanson answered like a man
"Thats what I aim to do."
But while he spoke the jam it broke
And Swanson he went through.

* * *

We drink our whiskey and our ale
And sweep the town just like a gale;
Then who comes to get us out of jail?
Louie Sands and Jim McGee.

* * *

So come all you jolly raftsmen with hearts stout and
    true
Don't depend on a woman; you're sunk if you do
And if you chance to meet one with dark chestnut
    curls,
Just think of Jack Haggerty and his Flat River girls.

* * *

On the banks of the Kettle River, among swamps
    and bogs
We've been busy all winter getting out logs.
To stay all winter is our design
And the firm we work for is called O'Brien.

Hurry up, boys, lets get done
Jobs nearly completed, we'll soon be gone
In years to come we'll all bear in mind
The years that we worked for Johnny O'Brien.

* * *

Then here's to the lumberjack, bad or good,
Who toils in the depth of the dark green wood.
Though rough of dress, of visage grim
Beneath it all there's a heart in him.

A sight of misery or want's appeal
He'll give his all for the sufferers weal
He's done his work well, the forest laid low
Soon, in story alone we'll the lumberjack know.

* * *

Simply put, they were proud of what they did and who
they were. They knew what mattered; they laughed at
what didn't. The world has few such singing workers
today. Muscle and bone against the wild make a man
proud and simple. The shantyboys started the legends in
Maine, the lumberjacks of the Lake States ended it. "In
story alone we them know."

By the 1890s, not all the jacks were the footloose, hell-
roarin', calk-stalking, bull-of-the-woods, fightin',
whorin', drunken sons of the Bangor Tigers, quick of
foot and ready for battle. The immigrant Swedes, Norwegians, and Finns in the woods and the Germans and
Poles in the mills came first to America, the land of opportunity, and second to white pine lumbering. They
often brought families with them, homesteaded, spent
winters felling pine, and returned to farm and family in
the spring. Their "pine logs" (wives and sweethearts)

waited for the long winter to end and for the farm, the
mill job, carpentry, or furniture making to bring their
men home for good. Their sons and daughters could see
that the pine would run out, that the end was in sight,
and they dreamed new and different dreams, dreams
that produced doctors, lawyers, teachers, and gradually,
as a new awareness developed, foresters bent on growing
anew what had fallen to make them what they were.
Sometimes by the light of the glim, the kerosene lamp, a
jack would read of home, and that night "lights out" was
a time of lonely darkness. Mail days were a mixed bless-
ing. Agnes Larson, a historian of white pine logging in
Minnesota, gives us some sense of these new jacks. "One
lumber jack told . . . (me) . . . of a Christmas Eve when
he, then a seventeen year old lad who had just come
from a home of refinement in Norway, was holding his
first job in America in the pine woods near Bemidji,
Minnesota. After the meal on that evening, always so
festive at home, he went out into the deep forest calling
his mother's name and weeping like a child." And so
began an American dream that would involve losing a leg
to a rolling log, a belated high school education, college,
a doctorate in economics, and a professorship at a college
schooling the sons and daughters of sodbusters and lumberjacks.

But while a new generation of woodsmen was beginning to settle in, to put down their roots in the country
they cut over or on the prairie farms near it, while families were growing so that at Christmas some jacks left
camp to return to "their families and kiddies left early in
fall, with the understanding that at Christmas they
would all be united again," the lumberjack of legend and
lore, the whiskey fighter, the loner who spent the winter's wages on a spree with wild, wild women, who "if
the ocean were whiskey and he were a duck, 'ud dive to
the bottom and never come up," still lived to foster
legends. The new nation created him in its own image.
First and foremost, he was a "working fool." His code
demanded "unslacking, prodigious toil." As Moonlight
Harry Schmidt, the last of the jacks in Michigan's
Upper Peninsula said, "They worked all day from the
first light until deep into night; they'd work their heart
out for you." Each man wanted to be the best swamper,
sawyer, axman, undercutter, or top loader in camp. And
each man wanted to work at the best camp, the camp
that hauled the most logs. Once the ice roads came,
every camp made its own "world's fair load," a record
load of 35,000 feet of white pine logs on a single sleigh.
Each camp's photo album shows a similar load. They bet
on their stamina, on their bone and muscle. An Iron
County jack bet he could "fell, limb, cut into four foot
lengths, split and pile a cord of hardwood in an hour."
He did it with six minutes to spare.

The new nation also wanted a brawler, a man of the
wild like his contemporary the cowboy and his predeces-

sor the mountain man, who was as willing to fight as he was to work; and the jacks obliged. The fights were legendary. They fought one another as often as not, and the rules required that no grudges be held. As Richard Dorson, a chronicler of lumberjack lore, says, the fights were "tests of valor," a proof of toughness. Winning or losing wasn't as important as being willing. It was a tradition that made two generations of doughboys the best infantrymen of the modern era. And the new nation expected the frontiersmen to be free-spending, free-living, unfettered by the restraints of civilization, caring not for tomorrow. The jacks fit the bill again. They "blew in" the winter's wages on one spree with "whiskey and wild, wild women." The ritual at the end of the season required the "well-heeled" jack to roar "Come on, boys, belly up to the bar." More imaginative variations were sometimes heard. "Balance two and how do yedo, and away goes Barney Waters. Come on, boys, and we'll snow the road. I'm foreman over all foremans. Give the boys another snort."

The jacks' exploits with ladies of the night were equally legendary, and towns like Muskegon, Hurley, and Duluth-Superior catered to the jacks' appetites. In Muskegon in 1887 at a wild Fourth of July spree, when the town was full of jacks after an enormous drive had buried the sawmills in logs, the ladies paid to build a pavilion eighty-four by one hundred and twenty, roofed the pavilion with boughs of pine and cedar, hired two bands, and received a thousand jacks who kicked off their calks; members of the sisterhood, as Holbrook calls them, arrived from Grand Rapids, Milwaukee, and Chicago to assist the Muskegon ladies in dancing the riverhogs down. And down they went as the whiskey and beer took their toll. The gala event was not repeated, since some of the "civilized" folk of Muskegon felt free living and free spending were fine as long as they stayed indoors.

But even though the jack was expected to raise holy hell when he had money in his pocket, like all American heroes he was to be decorous and respectful when in the presence of women "outside the profession." When meeting the teacher or being visited at camp by Sisters of Charity, the jacks did what all men of the wild since Natty Bumpo have done. They talked softly, gave to charity, doffed their hats, avoided profanity, and were, to use the appropriate term, gentlemen. In all of this, the legend and the reality blur, and undoubtedly alcoholism, venereal disease, murder, and mayhem were a part of the real world of the white pine lumbermen, as they have been for all the lonely outcasts who were in the vanguard of European civilization's encounter with the New World. But there was little hypocrisy in it all, and in the end few suffered save the jacks and their ladies. The civilization built its houses and churches out of their living, loving, and dying.

There was in each year a rhythm to the way of the pines and the men who lived by the felling of trees. If it ended in one or another of the barrooms and brothels from Seney to St. Louis, it always began in November in one of a hundred towns from Menominee to Bemidji. The returning jacks and the immigrant tenderfeet arrived by boat, train, oxcart, horseback, or foot, and the man catcher began to put together and dispatch the teams to the camps. The first in camp were the felling crews — the swampers, sawyers, and skidders. They arrived in November, and the first tasks involved siting and clearing the banking grounds where the cut logs would wait until the waters reached a driving pitch. Eventually, timber would be piled here in rollways, arranged so that with strategic blows of a sledge, the winter's cut could be dumped into the driving stream. The roads to the landing then had to be laid out and cleared. The foremen, working with years of knowledge, ran the ice-road routes so there were no uphills, and downhills were as gradual as possible through the heart of all the stands to be cut that winter. The swampers, following orders, began the task of clearing the roads. If the camp was a new one, the crew started earlier, and the swampers also built the bunkhouse, offices, stables, sheds, and cookhouse, living in tents until that task was done.

In the meantime, the sawyers and skidders began felling the trees according to the plan developed by the foreman in consultation with the company's cruiser. Choosing which trees to cut, laying out the roads, and directing the crews were the tasks that made the reputations of the camp bosses. The foreman who selected wisely, laid out his roads with maximum efficiency, and coordinated his swampers, sawyers, and skidders had his camp ready for the teamsters before Christmas. Once the ice-road traffic began moving, the camp was in full operation, and the longer the camp operated the larger the cut. The roadwork was crucial in this regard. Ice roads, unlike Maine oxen skid roads, had to be cleared of all roots and rocks. The horses needed roads free of such obstructions if they were to pull 15,000 to 20,000 feet of logs on each sleigh. Here the camp boss needed nature's cooperation as well. Snow and cold were crucial. The road could only be iced properly if enough snow had fallen and had been packed down. Occasionally, when thaws or heavy work wore the ruts through and no snow fell, the jacks would have to manufacture a "Swedish snowstorm" by hauling snow to patch the ice road. A sleigh with runners heated by steam was then pulled through the ruts to turn snow to ice. Once the cutting plan was made and the roads, landings, and banking ground ready, the daily cycle of camp life and the real job of the winter began.

Before dawn, the foreman leads his crew out. The axmen undercut the trees, and the sawyers begin. They wield seven-foot saws, slightly curved on the cutting edge, with a straight back slightly thicker than the cutting edge. When these saws replaced the ax, production jumped. As the saws start to sing, the teamsters begin to pick up the logs that skidding teams have brought to landings at the end of the previous day. With the horses stamping in the cold, two loaders and a top loader roll the enormous logs up onto the sleigh, piling them ten to twelve feet high. Two log rails are placed against the sleigh or against the logs already loaded. The sixteen-foot section to be loaded is rolled up the rails by the loaders using cant hooks. The top loader waits for the log to come to him. Calling instructions to his teammates to speed or slow their ends of the log, he plants his own cant hook, and with thrust of arms, back, and legs drops the rolling log into place on the load. It is a job requiring experience, timing, and great strength. Mistakes usually mean broken bones. If a log is without taper, the problems are not as great. But if a "blue" — a log bigger at one end than at the other — is coming up the rails, the top loader needs every skill at his command. He calls for a "Saginaw," and the groundhog retards the large end; he calls for a "St. Croix," and the groundhog helps the small end to gain. If the log is gummed — if the ends aren't even — as the blue hits the top of the load, the sky hooker Saginaws or St. Croixs himself. Cracked stems (broken legs) are common, and blues produce more than their share.

While the loading is proceeding, the first of the day's trees sways; and from first one side, then another, "Timber-r-r!" Then the explosions as the giants shake the earth with their fall. And the seven-foot saws sing again, now bucking the trees into sixteen-foot lengths. As the sawyers move on to the next tree, the skidding crews chain the logs to the go-devils, and horses pull the sixteen-footers to the nearest ice-road landing. There a decker or the rigging gang piles the logs to wait for the sleigh and the loading gang. The tasks are similar — bend the back, straighten the legs, throw your weight into the cant dog, and she'll move. The next skidding team arrives as the log drops in place.

By now its sleigh is loaded and the team strains into the traces. The load begins its journey to the banking ground. At downhills, the hayman-on-the-hill throws hay or sand in the ruts, and if the hill is steeper, uses the snubbers, devices for braking the sleigh. The sleighs have grown in size by 1890. Maine loggers had used a sleigh with a six-foot bunk. The bunks grew to eight, twelve, fourteen, and sixteen feet. A sixteen-foot bunk could accommodate 15,000 to 20,000 feet of logs weighing 150,000 to 200,000 pounds. Two- or four-horse teams pull the sleighs to the round turn, a circular track at the banking ground. The loaders go into action again, repeating their performance in reverse, and then stacking the logs in twenty-foot piles at the rollway. Again the sky hooker skillfully spins a ton of log into place to top off

the pile, and loaders and sleigh head upland, back to the landings for the next load.

At the banking ground, the scaler turns to estimating the load just delivered. His method is straightforward. Using his cheat stick, he measures the diameter of the log. A sixteen-inch-diameter log in sixteen-foot lengths scales 144 board feet, a twenty-eight incher, 576 feet, a thirty-six incher, 1,024 feet. A large cork log measuring forty-eight inches scales at 1,600 board feet. The scaler records each log's size in board feet. This bank scale not only provides the lumbermen with a measure of how many feet of lumber are being cut and sent to them, but establishes how much is cut from each piece of land and the price that will be paid to the drivers for the logs they will ride to the mills. As the scaling proceeds, a swamper wielding the branding axes marks each log with bark marks and stamp marks. The marks are registered with the state surveyor of logs and settle arguments about property rights. They enable bankers to hold liens on the logs and unpaid jacks to claim their pay in wood. The stamp mark is pounded into the end of each log with a branding ax. Bark marks are made with deft ax strokes in several different places on the log. They will be seen no matter how the log floats as the drive hits the booms. The marks look like hieroglyphics, combining the alphabet with intricate signs, figures, and characters indicating the owner's name, the piece of property where the tree was cut, and the season in which it was cut. A single company might have more than fifty registered marks. Scalers, river drivers, and boomers will read the hundreds of marks at a glance and send the right logs to the right mills. The pace is quickening; money must be made; logs can't be lost or stolen; and the clerk, the scaler, and the swampers recording and marking are part of the way of the pine in the 1890s. This is business, big business, billions of board feet and millions of dollars. The saws singing, the cant hooks chunking, the chains rattling, the harnesses jingling, and the branding axes thudding home. It is the way the day sounds until the thaws come and the ice roads turn to mud.

Before the spring drive begins, the crews take to the rivers and streams, cutting brush on the banks, removing windfalls, building dirt walls to hold the water high, making dams to hold water and to build up the head needed to carry the logs down the smaller streams. The crews build a wall of logs across the mouth of the swamp and spin them off when the rollways are ready. Later there will be sluice gates that can be raised and lowered as needed. On the lakes in the upper reaches of Michigan, Minnesota, and Wisconsin, the sleighs run their loads out onto the ice; as breakup nears, a boom of chained logs circles the piles. As the ice goes, the logs are ready for towing. Horse headworks accomplish the task. A sea anchor is rowed ahead of the headworks a thousand feet and dropped. The horses circle the windlass on the raft and pull the headworks and the boomed logs to the anchor. The anchor is raised, the process repeated. Horses rest in the stalls built on the raft, men in the workroom. And so they moved the logs to railheads, driving streams, or mills in the lake country of the North.

By the 1890s, the pattern of driving has changed. Initially, each company drove its own logs, but the time of specialization is at hand. Driving companies are formed "to handle all the logs on a river; (improving) efficiency and economy." It is Weyerhaeuser and the Chippewa Log and Lumber Company on the Black and Chippewa, the Saginaw boys and the St. Louis Drive and Improvement Company on the St. Louis in the Duluth District, and Weyerhaeuser and the Mississippi River Lumber Company through St. Anthony Falls on the Mississippi and rafting on to Rock Island and points south. So the drivers break the rollways and the winter's cut roars into the water. And once again the riverhogs run. Their style hasn't changed. As long as it lasts, into the first third of the twentieth century, the drive still demands that a man take the ultimate risk, run the rapids with death, freeze, stay wet continuously, and work all hours. As one of them said, "A man that can stand the log drive and not get sick need have no fears of death by sickness or exposure. Some accident must happen to him, or I think he will live on through the ceaseless years of eternity." But the chill reaches the bone, and the drivers drink hot whiskey when they first hit town. Many never make town; as the driving season opens, the papers of lumber country chant a litany of death. April 13 — "During the past week five men drowned on the Chippewa . . . "; April 15 — "This week five more drowned and one man broke his leg driving logs on . . . "; April 24 — "Three men drowned and many others were seriously injured when a jam of 50,000,000 feet broke . . ." And so the casualties are counted — no names, just numbers.

Now three crews work the drive. The driving crew runs with the head of the drive, keeping channels open. They spread themselves along the stream over ten- to fifteen-mile stretches, rolling forward as the jam crew catches them. They fight to keep the logs out of shoals and in the main stream. They leap into the rapids to twist a three-footer weighing a half ton off the rock it is hung on. Hear it in their own words. Hear Ben Harcourt, a jack of the Upper Peninsula.

> . . . Say this river is wide enough so that a jam say a 1½ million feet of timber in it would nicely fill about two miles of the river, we'll say that this drive has a lot of big logs timber in it that takes plenty of water to float, well parts of this river are peaces of water that are called riffles where the water is wavie going over rocks and if the water was a little shalliour it would hit these rocks and break and that is what the old time rivermen called white water, Well a big log will hit one of these rocks and hang up Maybe half way through the Riffles other logs coming down will hit this log and hang there with it and would cause what you'd call a wild center and it wouldn't be long till there would be a bad jam unless it was taken care of right away well as soon as the first big log got hung up the men would have to find some way of getting out to that log and roll it lose and send it down the river.

Ben goes on to tell us that the problem was the logs would keep hanging up, and if the crew wasn't able to keep up with the logs, the two miles of logs would jam into a one-eighth mile of river. The jam crew had to handle such problems. If the jam crew didn't break up the jam, either floodwaters built up and produced tremendous pressure which would send rampaging water and wood down the river or the water escaped and the logs were left high and dry. On the St. Louis in bad years, logs piled up bank to bank for six miles, twenty to thirty feet deep. On the St. Croix in the spring of 1886, 150,000,000 feet of logs piled up. It took two hundred riverhogs working twenty-four hours a day for six weeks to break the jam. Hear Ben Harcourt again.

> Well breaking a jam of this kind is what the story writers like to write about they make it look dangerious which it would be for anybody that wasent experienced and the fore man would see to it that if a man was green at the job wouldent be working where it was dangerous. Well the face of this jam would be 12 to 16 feet high from the river bed up piled in all kinds of shap, the men would start in on one side close to the bank with there peaveys theyed pry and lift and bull to get a few logs loose so they could get a small channel back through the jam the water is running through the jam all the time so as they loosen a log it floats a way they'll work this way till they get a channel 3 or 4 rods into the jam and clean out the logs next to the bank so there'll be nothing binding and soon the logs will start looseing up from the bottom and pritty soon the whole jam would start hauling logs would turn end over end and logs a foot through snap and break in two like you'd break a match with your fingers, as logs would role down in to the deeper water below the rapids they would melt and spred out and continieued down the river the crew would be out on the logs with there Pike poles and peaveys helping the logs along so that they wouldent jam any more till they got thined out in good shap, Well I just gave you a good discription of one of your dangerious jams I'v worked on more than one such jam and I never happen to be working the River where anybody was ever Killed or drowned all though such things have happened."

For brave Ben and the other rivermen it was simply a job. It is the writers who see it another way. Otis W. Terpening sang this homage.

Straight up from the edge of the river
Where the tall whispering Hemlock still waves,
In a cool shady nook of the forest
I first saw the river Jacks grave
In the shade of a Hemlock they laid him
Where the sweet fern and maden hair bends.

Just a circle of pebbles to mark it
Placed there by the hands of friends,
He died on the drive, so they told me
Went under with peavy in hand,
Still holding it tight when they found him
Halfburied in water and sand.

All day he'd worked like a madman
On a wing jam that formed at the bend,
All day unafraid he had faced it
And was faceing it still at the end,
No chance to escape when it started
'Twas swift as the thrush of a knife.

He had gambled, with death as the forfeit
And was paying the debt with his life,
Not for fame nor fortun he struggled
'Twas simple the part of the game,
But friends, if he wasent a hero
Then no one is worthy the name.

Behind the jam crew the work goes on. The rear crew tracks down strays, pulling them out of inlets, swamps, and sloughs. Their job is known as sacking. They work in the water, wet through, day after day, working often alone thirty to forty miles behind the driving crew, fighting mud, sand, and current to get every hung log afloat. A large bateau, thirty-five feet long, carries the crew back and forth across the river picking up and dropping off a man or two wherever the logs are hung. Is it any wonder they dreamed and sang of "Hot whiskey, Hot whiskey, I cried. If I don't get hot whiskey I surely will die."

And how they moved wood. A good drive in the 1870s saw 50 men bring 12,000,000 feet down the St. Croix. At the end of the century, 150 men drove 60,000,000 feet down the Mississippi. Tens of thousands of river-hogs rode the white pine out of the edge of night in Michigan, Wisconsin, and Minnesota every year during the golden age of white pine lumbering. And they ate when they could, ashore or in the wanigan, slept when they could on the cold bosom of the riverbank even as the frost was leaving that hard ground. In a clear year, the jams were few and small, the logs came down floating high, and each man drank his hot whiskey hoping he'd never be on a "River where anybody was ever Killed or drowned although such things happened."

Things were quieter at the booms. The business of lumbering required the sorting of logs the driving companies had brought down the rivers. A typical boom works consisted of "a long holding boom with a gap to allow the logs to pass. Extending from the gap were two parallel lines at booms, making a long watery avenue down which the logs floated. The side booms were broken at regular intervals, and behind each opening was a log pen. Men standing on the side boom reached out with twenty-foot pike poles and pulled logs into the pens, logs with the same mark being rafted" in each pen. In the 1890s, Weyerhaeuser and his associates moved the largest and most famous booming operation in the pineries from the Beef Slough to the West Newton Slough. The Beef Slough boom owed its fame to the twenty-year battle of words and laws that made Fredric Weyerhaeuser and the Mississippi River Lumber Company. The West Newton boom across the river from the Beef Slough was built because the felling of the giants along the Black, the Chippewa, the St. Croix, and the Mississippi was having its effects, and the slough once capable of floating logs was filling with the silt running off millions of acres of cutover pineland. The West Newton Slough could still float logs, and the boom there operated past the turn of the century.

Once the logs were at the boom, the task was to scale, sort, and raft them. Since an individual company had many log marks, the first task was identification. As soon as the logs were in the holding boom, a catchmarker "corked" across the top of the logs with ax in hand, tally board in pocket. Reading the log marks, occasionally birling a log to find a clearer mark, and noting the several different marks — marks for loggers, landowners, and millowners could all be on a single log — the catchmarker brought order out of chaos. He swung the ax, cut a new sign, renamed the many-named, and set the catchmark on top for all to see. Now sorters and scalers took their turn and walked the catwalks measuring and moving the logs down "the long lanes, from the main race to the pockets where they awaited the rafting gang." One mark to a pocket, several pockets per firm, the wood was ready to move to the mills.

By the 1890s, log rafting had become mechanized. Muscle and bone gave way to steam. The riverboat, the towboat, had totally replaced current-driven, sweep-directed rafts. And the rafts had grown in size. The raft pilot was now at the helm of the towboat, and his crew worked on deck with steam-driven capstans to turn the raft through the twisting channels of the Mississippi. The evolution of new techniques and technology spread from the end of the Civil War to the turn of the century and was the crucial transportation development in feeding the ever-growing demand of the Mississippi Valley mills. By the 1890s, the towboats were specially designed and extremely powerful. They pushed the logs much as barges were pushed. Since the 1880s, the rafts themselves had been formed by encasing them in overlapping boom sticks which were held together by chains. The booms were held against the logs by a quarter-inch wire cable "stretched tightly across each brail from boomstick to boomstick." Forty to sixty feet wide, these were the basic unit of the log rafts of the 1890s.

Piloting the raft boat required all the skill of the raft pilots of the early years. In fact, some men moved from sweeps to steam. The raft-boat pilot used his rudders, and when the occasion demanded, he used his entire boat to turn the immense rafts, steering them into the clear channels. Rafts reached three quarters of a mile in length and were limited in width only by the bridge spans that now crossed the Father of Waters at site after site. The bridges, as they sprang into shape, finished the free-floating rafts. Bone and muscle couldn't cut it quite as fine as steam could. Even steam wasn't enough until the pilot knew every twist the flexible raft could make as capstan and rudders worked. Stephen Hanks, Lincoln's brother and "dean of the raft pilots," who floated rafts from the earliest days, in his first tow hit bridges at Burlington, Iowa, Keokuk, Illinois, and Quincy, Illinois. Eventually, he became one of the most skillful pilots on the river. Finally, rafting in the 1890s developed a new method of dealing with the treacherous upper and lower rapids on the Mississippi. As the raft approached the rapids, a second boat was tied off sideways against the front of the raft. With whistle signals, the raft pilot directed the "bow" boat forward and back, left and right, or stopped and dead ahead, and wound three quarters of a mile of white pine through the narrow twisting rapids. Special rapids pilots guided the rafts through these sections of churning, rock-lined riffles and white water. Steam, winches, bow boats, and specialization moved 847,443,200 feet of logs in 1893. A river of white pine flowed to Rock Island, Keokuk, and St. Louis; fortunes were made; the prairies were populated. Illuminated by the new electric lights, the saws at the mills howled through the night.

What made the mills howl was steam — steam and speed. The mills of the Lake States were changing faster than any other part of the white pine business. First, saws changed from the muley cutting 5,000 feet a day to the circulars and gang saws cutting 4,000 feet an hour to the band saws cutting 10,000 feet an hour. Speed wasn't the only thing; the millowners of the 1880s and 1890s were concerned about wastage. A circular saw or a gang saw cut a quarter-inch kerf, and that meant one one-inch board was wasted for every four produced. The band saw cut an eighth-inch kerf, wasting one board for every eight produced. At ten dollars a thousand, the difference for a mill producing 100,000 feet a day might mean one hundred dollars. Economy, efficiency, and speed, speed, speed.

The saws taxed the ability of all the other equipment. Edgers couldn't keep up, so new ones were invented which edged both sides of the board at once. The log carriage that fed the logs into the saws was hand oper-

ated at first, then mechanized, then speeded. The logs were loaded from the boom by hand, then a bull chain, a chain with sharp lugs attached, pulled the logs from boom to saw. In milling a log, the log had to be turned to position it properly to yield the maximum number of boards from each log. This too was done by hand until the steam nigger began "in the blink of a second to turn half-ton logs as though they were saplings." As the lumber flew out of the new saws fed by bull chains, steam niggers, and automated carriages, the millhands and the off-bearers who were to pile the sawed lumber were being buried by a stream of white pine. The solution was simple — roller systems called live rolls carried the logs to and lumber from the saws. And it all went faster, faster, faster. Waterpower was, in fact, a bit too slow, and once millowners found that burning sawdust and shavings could produce steam and rid them of waste, even the economic advantages of waterpower vanished. More and more it was steam and speed. In the 1870s, big mills cut 100,000 feet a day. In the 1880s, it was 200,000, and by the 1890s, 250,000.

The process of drying the wood also changed. Green saw lumber could not be shipped as profitably as dry because of its moisture content. The usual practice until the 1880s was to air dry the lumber. The process took about a year, depending on moisture conditions. The dry kiln shortened the process to weeks, and the excess steam of the mills provided all the heat needed. All in two decades, as quickly as each became available, nigger, live rolls, planing mills, tramways for carrying cut lumber, kilns, automatic firing of engines with sawdust, smoke consumers, bull chains, band saws, double gangs. And that wasn't the end of it. Lake States lumbering saw the development of hot ponds, log-holding areas adjacent to the mills with steam lines run into them to keep them from freezing in saw logs until spring. The mills needed to run year round, and run they did, hot ponds and all. And if the mills could run in winter, the jacks could fell in summer. The crews had grown larger and more men were in the woods, but some means to move the sixteen-foot logs was needed. First it was Big Wheels, five feet from hub to rim, ten feet in diameter. The axle rode above the stumps; logs could roll through the summer and did. But top loading was slow and so the jammer, a crane that lifted logs on the sleighs and rail cars, was born. At first, jammers were horse powered, but by the turn of the century, steam lifted the logs. The Horace Butters' Patent Skidding and Loading Machine wasn't ready until 1886, and by then there wasn't enough time or pine left in the Lake States. The Butters' skidders would drag yellow pine in the South and Douglas fir and redwood in the West, but it was too late for white pine.

The mills were generally two-story buildings, built at riverfront. The logs were bull chained from the boom to the second-floor saw rooms. Each mill contained two howling circular saws, with log carriages sliding back and forth on short tracks paralleling the saws. Opposite, the gang saw swallowed two logs at a time and spit out one-inch boards, the logs rocking slightly as they trundled on into the gang, live rolling out to the gang edgers and cutoff saws. The skins, the bark, and the sapwood fell onto more live rollers and wound their way to the furnaces to fuel the dissections of the bodies of their kin, to speed the process of building a better tomorrow. And so it went from machine to machine, from speed to speed. There were prices to be paid. All the machines showed a colossal indifference to the men who fed them wood. Saws, niggers, live rolls, and bull chains claimed limbs and lives. Jackets were caught by rotating shafts, bodies pulled into blind steel teeth, slasher saws, and ripsaws. Arms and fingers were lost as blood lubricated the bearings and helped to slide the wood home.

And what did these workers earn for arms, legs, blood, and death? In the woods, foremen on their way to becoming lumbermen — dealers in wood, millowners, log owners — earned up to $1,800 a year. Cooks and teamsters were paid $40 to $70 a month, sawyers $35, top loaders $35, others $20 to $30 or less. After paying for purchases at the camp store, Andrew Olson, having worked 104 days, left camp with $93.55. C. H. Peterson worked 98 days to bring home $79.44. Tom Anthony worked from November 16 to March 31, earning $124.90, spent $32.95 for socks, a blanket jacket, tobacco and sundries, and received a bill of time for $91.85. He could collect his $91.85 after the logs were at the mill on August 15, 1888. And so the Olsons, Swansons, Petersons, and their Maine, Finnish, German, and French-Canadian cousins sometimes spent their summers working in the mills with their Polish and German colleagues. In 1889, if the jack worked 9.9 months in woods and mill, on the average he would earn $474.43 — a sum that included the cost of food furnished in the lumber camp. The average daily wage in the woods was $1.86 in 1889/90. Foremen earned $2.40 a day, cooks $2.00, swampers $1.25. The mill workers' salaries on the average were between $1.25 and $2.50 per day, with $1.83 being the average wage. Mills employed 50 to 350 men. There was a superintendent, a boom master, a yardmaster, a mill foreman, a chief engineer with assistants, sawyers, lumber checkers, saw filers, scalers, shipping clerks, yardmen, and laborers. They worked as long as there were logs to saw, ten to eleven hours a day. And by the 1890s, they'd begun to think about unions and strikes. By the time they were organized, the white pine was gone and with it the jobs they'd had. Most managed to get their stake, prove their homestead, settle in. Those who didn't moved west with Weyerhaeuser, met the Wobblies, and came to know the ways of the new age. But among the pine it was "bust your gut for a dollar a day" and "owe your soul to the company store."

And out of their labor, out of the movements of ice and water, out of the grinding of rocks, out of the bodies of the pines, the rugged individualists were building a nation and their fortunes. In 1887, Weyerhaeuser was making lumber at Rock Island, Chippewa Falls, Shell Lake, Baronet, Mason, Hayward, and at Knife Falls on the St. Louis. Three years later, he purchased the Northern Pacific Land Grant in Minnesota and moved to St. Paul. Two years after that, he bought Wright-Davis holdings and 50,000,000 feet of stumpage from the St. Paul and Duluth Railroad Company. Prices on pineland were being driven up, and only Weyerhaeuser and his syndicate could meet the new prices. He next bought out 75,000 acres from the St. Anthony Lumber Company for $1,710,000 dollars (roughly $170,000,000 in 1980 dollars). It took the syndicate cruiser 114 days working with a large crew to estimate the timber involved in the purchase. The Mississippi River Lumber Company was born. Before his life ended, Weyerhaeuser would own major shares of, and preside over, Potlatch Lumber and the Pine Tree Lumber Company purchased from Backus and Brooks and would operate mills in Minneapolis, Little Falls, Cloquet, Virginia. He closed his Minnesota operation with the Virginia and Rainy Lake Company. As the century turned, Fredric Weyerhaeuser, who had followed the edge of night north and west, organized the Weyerhaeuser Timber Company, buying 900,000 acres in western Washington. The company increased its holdings steadily for the next decade and then moved into Oregon. It owned pine in Idaho and invested in short-leaf and long-leaf pine in Louisiana, Arkansas, and Mississippi. Weyerhaeuser was president of twenty-one companies in 1902, was on the board of directors of the Chicago Great Western Railroad, and had interests in the Merchants National Bank of St. Paul, the Continental and Commercial National Bank of Chicago, the Third National Bank of St. Louis, and the First National Bank of Duluth. The jacks cut and loaded, the riverhogs danced and drove, the boomers poled and birled, the raft pilots ruddered and whistled, the saws whined, and the kilns hissed. The army of light moved, and Fredric Weyerhaeuser, immigrant millhand, owned the woods. The dominion of the pines had built a kingdom, made a captain of industry. The golden age of white pine lumbering was past, the broadleafs would inherit the earth, the jacks and mills would move west. A way of life was passing.

And it ended by moving away from water, into the plains on steel and steam. As Duluth district pine began to flow east down the lakes and Canadian white pine logs began to be towed in bag booms to Michigan mills, at the western edge, the last edge of the pine night, another story was unfolding. T. B. Walker and company were crossing the divide. Leaving St. Anthony Falls, Walker entered the Northwest Slope, whose waterways flowed north to Hudson's Bay. Walker built his sawmill at Crookston, Minnesota, where pine met prairie, and by 1889 Crookston was the "center for the greatest wheat producing region in the world and Sawdust City." In that year, Walker's mill produced 45,000,000 feet of white pine and paid $216,000 in salaries. His wood went into the Dakotas, on past the Missouri riding the Northern Pacific, and north and west on the Manitoba Line. Walker saw the end of the Mississippi pine and moved into a new region to supply a new market; rails were the key to opening the way west for people, pine, and an industry. They were also the way to the last of the pine. Along the northern edge of the Lake States, the last of the pine were remote from streams that flowed east and south, unavailable to loggers until railroads provided a means of moving logs to mill or mill to logs. And so the mop-up action in the broadleaf campaign rode steel into the remaining vestiges of night. It had begun with the Lake George and Muskegon, and the Flint and Pere Marquette in Michigan in the mid-seventies. As the 1890s unfolded and the century turned, the rails began to reach into the last bastion of the retreating pines. The Duluth, South Shore & Atlantic Railway along the northern edge of the Upper Peninsula, Duluth to Sault Ste. Marie, the Soo Line Railroad down the North Shore of Lake Michigan through northern Wisconsin to Minneapolis, the Milwaukee Lake Shore & Western Railway through Ashland to Lake Michigan, the Northern Pacific Railway through Minnesota from Duluth to the prairies, the Wisconsin Central Railway, the Chicago-Minneapolis & Omaha Railway, the Great Northern Railway, the Duluth & Iron Range Railroad, the Duluth, Missabe & Iron Range Railway, the Itasca Lumber Company Road, the Duluth, Mississippi & Northern Railway. They carried the logs to mill or driving stream.

In 1895, the railroad logs at Swan River — the railhead for the Itasca Lumber Company — were piled on the river "twenty-five and thirty tiers high almost the entire width of the stream and the logs filled a full mile of the Mississippi." The Brainerd & Northern Railway went sixty miles north from Brainerd to Leech Lake and kept ten locomotives and five hundred logging cars moving wood to their electrically lighted log landing in Brainerd. The Chippewa River & Menominee Railway ran from Verona to Weyerhaeuser, Wisconsin, a short twelve miles. Two locomotives were used, one for switching and the other to move five trains through the working areas of thirteen logging contractors and several camps of the Mississippi River Logging Company. Eight hundred men worked the cuttings, and the Chippewa filled with logs. They cut fifteen million feet of logs a month.

As the logs moved by rail to mills and driving streams,

curious exchanges began to occur. The rivers controlled logging before the railroad era; now the railroads could carry logs and lumber anywhere in any direction. In a final burst of mechanical wizardry, the agents of the broadleafs finished the pines, taking them at will, moving the giants in all directions at once. The dominion of man had come. The Duluth, Mississippi & Northern brought St. Louis River logs to the Mississippi. Railroads carried logs from the Rainy River and Lake of the Woods region away from Canadian mills to Virginia and Duluth. Railroads carried Red River logs away from Winnipeg across the Northwest Slope to the Mississippi and sent them on their way to St. Louis. The Empire Lumber Company linked the St. Croix to Dedham, Wisconsin, and trees cut fifteen miles from Lake Superior were hauled to the St. Croix, driven to Stillwater, rafted to Winona. At the same time, logs were being hauled out of the St. Croix Valley to Ashland on Lake Superior and then south to the Chippewa River milling center at Eau Claire. Logs were hauled from the St. Croix eastward to Rhinelander on the Wisconsin River. As the century turned, the Northern Pacific contracted to haul twenty million feet of logs to Stillwater, and the Topor Lumber Company shipped twelve million from north of Virginia, Minnesota, to Stillwater. There the logs were unloaded, rafted, and towed 450 miles to Keokuk.

Man and machine, knowledge and power; the broadleafs had chosen their allies wisely. The numbers grew. In 1904, Powers and Simpson at Hibbing had 900 men in the woods. In 1906, 2,000 men were working for C. A. Smith, the Pillsburys, T. B. Walker, and Weyerhaeuser at Cohasset. The specialists logged for all the lumbermen, and the mills screamed as the pine came by water or steel, east, west, north, south, upriver and down, across the divides. In 1895, 12,000 men worked for two hundred firms and individuals felling Minnesota pine. Five years later, 20,000 men worked cutting pine in three Minnesota counties — St. Louis, Itasca, and Beltrami. The kingdom of the pines, the edge of night, was growing small, the numbers of men were growing enormously, the machines, clanking and hissing, were in high gear.

Now there were steam log haulers to carry immense loads. Caterpillar tractors, steam skidders, donkey engines, locomotives, steam jammers, skylines, tail trees, bull blocks, chokers, crotch lines, ground leads, and haulbacks. A new language, a language of speed and power, a language that spoke little of hands and backs, much of grease, gasoline, and oil. But before Butters' skidder could be used, before the question of whether it's better to bring the wood to the mills or the mills to the woods could be answered, and long before chain saws and tree farmers, before Peterbilt and D-9, the white pine was gone. The Douglas fir, the redwoods, and the pines of the South will experience the final phases of this quest for more wood faster, as will, in the end, the momentarily victorious broadleafs. Their turn has come as the dominion of man reaches maturity. The bridges are across the rivers; the cities shine as stars over the face of the land. There is no night. The poor, the hungry, the downtrodden, the huddled masses, have come, they have seen, they have conquered.

Hauling logs with oxen in the 1880's over a "corduroy" road. These roads were prepared by laying logs across them in order for loads to pass over wet sections. *Courtesy, State Historical Society of Wisconsin.*

(Opposite page)
Looking down the St. Croix River in Wisconsin. *Courtesy, State Historical Society of Wisconsin.*

Loggers on logs stacked for transporting in northern Minnesota in the 1890's. *Courtesy, Minnesota Historical Society.*

(Opposite page, top)
"River hogs" taking time out to have their picture taken while rolling logs into a river in Michigan. *Courtesy, State Historical Society of Wisconsin.*

(Opposite page, bottom)
A log jam on the St. Croix River in 1886. *Courtesy, Minnesota Historical Society.*

A wanigan on the Mississippi River at St. Cloud in 1908. *Courtesy, Minnesota Historical Society.*

(Opposite page, top)
Bronson and Folsom Company rafting crew about 1896. Taken at the rafting grounds landing on the east side of Lake St. Croix across from Stillwater, Minnesota. *Courtesy, Minnesota Historical Society. Photo: John Runk.*

(Opposite page, bottom)
A small log jam on the Menominee River in Michigan. Note the small boat, called a "bateau" in the foreground. The bateau was commonly used during river drives in Michigan and Wisconsin. *Courtesy, Marquette County Historical Society.*

A common form of rafting on the larger midwestern rivers was to tie the logs together and move them, under steam power, downstream to major sawmills. This raft was photographed at Fulton, Illinois in July, 1901. *Courtesy, State Historical Society of Wisconsin.*

(Opposite page, top)
Up to 1860 the cut of logs coming through the St. Croix boom averaged between 50,000,000 and 60,000,000 feet each year. A few years later this was increased to 100,000,000 feet, then 180,000,000 and in 1880 to 200,000,000, steadily increasing up to 300,000,000 feet which was the annual average in 1888. This picture was taken at the St. Croix boom in 1886. *Courtesy, Minnesota Historical Society. Photo: John Runk.*

(Opposite page, bottom)
A "float" below the Kilbourne Dam in Wisconsin. Rivers were the major means by which logs were transported to the sawmills. Because of log jams, companies started tying their logs together to form long rafts or "floats". These were guided down the rivers by rafting crews manning long sweep oars. The rafts were often more than 100 feet long and the men would work, eat and sleep "on board". *Courtesy, State Historical Society of Wisconsin.*

The Dells on the St. Croix River in Wisconsin. This river was extremely important for transporting logs during the height of Wisconsin's lumbering era. *Courtesy, State Historical Society of Wisconsin.*

(Opposite page, top)
The "wanigan" or cook raft "Dancing Annie" at Eagle Rapids on the Chippewa River in 1909. The wanigan followed the log drives in the spring. Aboard was a crew to prepare meals for the log driving crews. *Courtesy, Minnesota Historical Society.*

(Opposite page, bottom)
Log jam at Chippewa Falls, Wisconsin, 1869. *Courtesy, State Historical Society of Wisconsin.*

97

Men turning out of their bunks on the "cook" raft. *Courtesy, State Historical Society of Wisconsin.*

(Opposite page, top)
Log rafts on the Wisconsin River. *Courtesy, State Historical Society of Wisconsin.*

(Opposite page, bottom)
Unplugging the gate at the Dells Dam on the Wolf River in Wisconsin. *Courtesy, Oshkosh Public Museum.*

A plug in the gate
at the
Dells Dam
on the
Wolf River

These logs were unloaded on the St. Croix River in the years of 1903 and 1904 by Bronson and Folsom Company. They were shipped here by rail from Virginia, Minnesota. In Stillwater the logs were made into rafts and taken down the Mississippi River. *Courtesy, Minnesota Historical Society. Photo: John Runk.*

(Opposite page, top)
Looking up the Eau Claire River in Wisconsin. *Courtesy, State Historical Society of Wisconsin.*

(Opposite page, bottom)
Fred P. Murphy riding a log through the flume over Second Falls on the Burnside River in northern Minnesota. These flumes were built to protect the logs as they went over the falls and also to prevent jamming. *Courtesy, Northeast Minnesota Historical Center.*

View of the Wisconsin River, an important log transportation route. *Courtesy, State Historical Society of Wisconsin.*

(Opposite page, top)
Log jam on the Cloquet River in Minnesota. *Courtesy, Northeast Minnesota Historical Center.*

(Opposite page, bottom)
Log dam at the Lower Falls of the Salmon Trout River in Michigan, 1890. *Courtesy, Marquette County Historical Society.*

Lumber schooner on the Chicago River, probably about 1900. *Courtesy, Chicago Historical Society, ICHi-05415.*

(Opposite page, top)
Loading a sail barge at the Scott Graff docks in Duluth, Minnesota in 1915. This lumber was shipped to Chicago, Buffalo and North Tonawanda, New York. From the years 1850 to 1926 there were approximately 7,250,000,000 feet of lumber shipped by water from the head of the lakes. During 1904, there were 473,000,000 feet shipped from Duluth alone. *Courtesy, Northeast Minnesota Historical Center.*

(Opposite page, bottom)
Loading logs at Knife River, Minnesota in the early 1900's. *Courtesy Northeast Minnesota Historical Center.*

The Charles B. Packard, built in 1887, photographed in 1905 while shipping railroad ties. *Courtesy, Milwaukee Public Library.*

(Opposite page, top)
A steamhauler. These steam powered tracked vehicles began to replace horses in the woods in the early 1900's. A driver sat up front to steer the skis while a fireman kept the steam up by firing the boiler with wood. A slow but powerful machine, the steamhauler could pull many loads of cut logs to a river bank or rail landing. *Courtesy, Marquette County Historical Society.*

(Opposite page, bottom)
A train ready to move out with a load of full length white pine logs in Black River, Michigan in 1884. *Courtesy, Marquette County Historical Society.*

With the coming of logging railroads, bridges, such as this one, had to be constructed over rivers and between hills. *Courtesy, Minnesota Historical Society.*

(Opposite page, top)
A steam hauler pulling a long line of loaded sleds. *Courtesy, Minnesota Historical Society.*

(Opposite page, bottom)
A logging train at Walker, Minnesota in 1896. *Courtesy, Minnesota Historical Society.*

A Brainerd Lumber Company logging train near Nisswa, Minnesota in 1901. *Courtesy, Minnesota Historical Society.*

(Opposite page, top)
Logging train in northern Minnesota in the early 1900's. *Courtesy, Northeast Minnesota Historical Center.*

(Opposite page, bottom)
A logging train with berry pickers in Wisconsin in the late 1890's. *Courtesy, Oshkosh Public Museum.*

Logs stacked in Knife River, Minnesota in preparation for their transportation down Lake Superior in 1910. *Courtesy, Minnesota Historical Society. Photo: William Roleff, Two Harbors, Mn.*

(Opposite page, top)
The train and the horse; without each, the midwestern timber industry could not have existed!
Courtesy, State Historical Society of Wisconsin.

(Opposite page, bottom)
These are log marks used by lumber companies to distinguish their logs from others' during log drives, at log booms and in the mill ponds at the sawmills. The marks were pounded into the ends of the logs using a steel stamper. *Courtesy, State Historical Society of Wisconsin.*

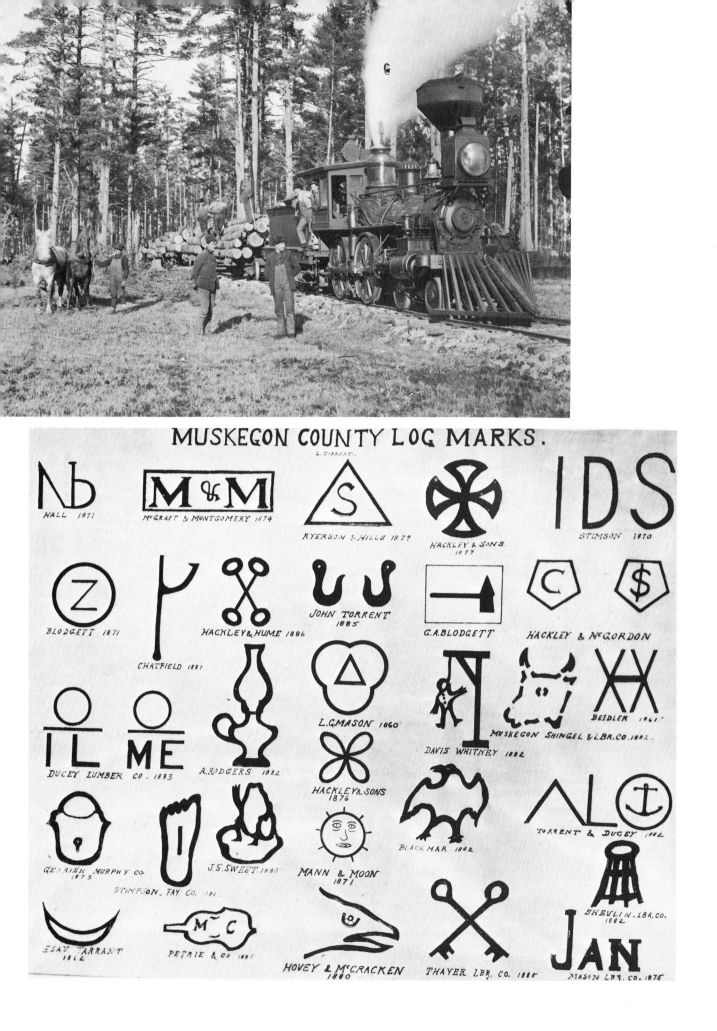

MUSKEGON COUNTY LOG MARKS.

Mature eastern white pine on the Menominee Indian Reservation in Wisconsin. To gain a sense of scale, note the person in the lower left hand corner. *Courtesy, State Historical Society of Wisconsin.*

CHAPTER FIVE

The Passing of the Pines:
The Lessons of Lumbering

AND WHAT ARE the lessons of the passing of the pine? Come travel a journey in the mind. Follow Lake County 2 north from Two Harbors on Lake Superior. Here you can see the last fell, the last stand. Up from the shore, rising over the headlands of Glacial Lake Duluth, past the Big Noise Tavern and the cutoff to Wales and Rollins, into the Superior National Forest, aspen trunks are turning from gray to green. The sap is rising; the cycle is beginning another turn. The many fingers of the Cloquet crossing Lake County 2 are high. Occasionally there is water on the road. Cross the Duluth, Missabe & Iron Range tracks. Imagine the beginning — trainloads of white pine running down to the Duluth mills from Isabella landing, down to build ore docks and elevators, forming a partnership of wood and steel, bringing the Zenith City's long-awaited boom. Next imagine the Reserve tracks to Beaver Bay, crossing the Duluth, Missabe & Iron Range east of the highway at Northshore Junction. Imagine the end, when Reserve runs its tracks to Beaver Bay and builds the world's first taconite plant. The plant pulls the Zenith City out of the bust everyone knew had to come. The pine is gone. The hematite is gone. Pulpwood and hardrock become a way of life. In the Superior National Forest, "logging" is left to do; "lumbering" is what you did when the pines had dominion, when saw logs were bucked at sixteen feet, when the headsaws howled, when timbers, boards, sash, and millwork were sorted and stacked along the waterfront. Now the cut is aspen, popple. Hauling truckloads of eight-foot sticks or semiloads of chips, chipped by the "Cat" chipper at the cut, out of the whole tree, snipped above the roots, or ripped out, roots and all, by the "Cat" tree farmer.

The woods rattle to the sounds of diesels and chain saws. Occasionally, you can hear a shout above the clatter of the machines. There is no singing; there are no camps. The men drive back and forth to the stumpage. Jackpine and spruce fall as well. The long-grain, high-resin softwoods are needed to ensure the proper mix in the papermaking soup at Potlatch's Cloquet Mills, at Superwood in Duluth, at Blandin in Grand Rapids, or at Boise Cascade in International Falls. Chipboard is the newest innovation. Sometimes it's simply called Blandex after the pioneering technologists at Blandin who found a way to glue the chipped trees back together into the preferred four-foot by eight-foot sheets. It's even cheaper than plywood, and will build the next generation of houses and garages. The chips make a pretty pattern, and the third generation panels rooms with reglued aspen. If you don't rip the roots out, aspen will be back twenty years after you've clipped and chipped. The president has ordered the United States Forest Service to raise production, and a spruce budworm epidemic has blasted large stands of black spruce. The second, third, and fourth growth is falling by order of man and God. But this is national forest. Tree planting and the aspen's capacity to regenerate new clones from its ancient roots will bring the woods back again for a sustained yield; wood is a renewable resource. Man and God cooperate in raising what has fallen.

Now look. Here just beyond the tracks, see what was — a few scattered on either side of the road, then more, denser, seventy-five feet, a hundred, a hundred and twenty. See a Forest Service sign — "White Pine Picnic Ground" — and a drive-through lane. Two of the ever-present, government outhouses, an interpretive sign, an explanation — these are white pine. They were alive when the Revolutionary War was being fought. The mind catches. Through the War of 1812. Through the Mexican War, the Civil War, the Spanish-American War, World War I, World War II. Alive through it all. Through Valley Forge, the Battle of New Orleans, Gettysburg, San Juan Hill, Argonne, Guadalcanal, Hiroshima, Pusan, Mai Lai. From the dominion of the pines to the dominion of man, alive. The columns rise behind the sign. The quiet rises up the trunks to the crowns. Under the trees there is more growth than expected. An understory waiting its turn. But here for two acres, by man's choice, they stand and remind us. Of what? What are they saying? "Here, man, but for the grace of, whatever, go you"? "This is what was and what is no more. Be ashamed"? No. This is not what is felt. There is quiet. There is a sense of loss, a kind of tenseness behind the eyes, a struggle to imagine, to see what must have been. You understand, it was never all pine. The alder, aspen, birch were always there; but so were the pine, billions of them. Between 1776 and 1940, two quadrillion, four hundred thousand million board feet of white pine were cut to build 52 million homes, 12 million farm houses, 2 million schools and libraries, 650,000 churches, and 450,000 factories. If all the lumber cut during that quarter of a millenium were piled on one city block, the pile would be four hundred miles high, roughly seventy-five mountains the height of Mt. Everest. Those seventy-five mountains of wood have housed the poor, made the landless landed, and built towns, cities, churches, and schools. Without the pine, no America. Without the pine, no freedom. The pine fell for us.

Now turn east by northeast on the Whyte Road, Forest Road 104. Drive the old rail grade past Railroad Lake, on to a "T" junction fifteen miles distant. Here and there, ties are still breaking through road surfaces, and the ride is rough. The country is black spruce swamp. Few except loggers visit the area. The lakes are small and scattered. There are no campgrounds, no iron mines, no resorts, no canoeable waters — only the old roads and the forests. Turn south on the Cloquet Lake Road, over the ties still under the roadbed. After three miles, turn east onto a dipping, twisting pathway, the Hefflefinger Truck Trail. No trains ran this road. This is a road built by a generation of truck loggers to reach the headlands above the west branch of the Baptism and the east branch of the Beaver. No state highway maps show this road to the past, to the old forest. After ten miles, turn east on an unnumbered, unnamed piece of logging trail running south to a ridge that separates the drainage basins of the Baptism and the Beaver, a headland for Lake Superior's glacial ancestor, Lake Duluth. It is high ground, well drained. Now at its highest point, walk up a path through a grove of sugar maple, companion species to the *Pinus strobus* of the Lake States, a broadleaf competitor. The trees are half as old as the pine of the picnic ground. See the sign marking a path through the maples — "Scenic Overlook." Follow the path up through the maples to an open rock face, scarred by the passing of the ice sheet. Look back at the maples and wonder. The tangle of spruce, popple, balsam, birch, hazelbrush,

alder, and willow gives way to trees standing alone amidst the litter of their own fallen limbs and leaves; it is climax vegetation, a rarity in the heavily logged forests of Minnesota's Arrowhead.

There are hints of maple along most of Lake Superior's North Shore, but they seem only decorative and incidental, as though nature were a painter or a gardener who occasionally wanted her birch-aspen golds broken by pink, orange, and red hues. But up-country six to ten miles, off the highway maps, along the highest ridges of the headlands from Duluth to Grand Marais, sugar maple stands crown steep, well-drained slopes. Unlike their lowland cousins the red maples, which share their ground with the densities of brush and evergreens, the sugar maples bury their rivals in gold and red. These broadleafs provided flooring and furniture, cornices and chopping blocks for a generation of lumbermen in Michigan, where the trees grew in large enough quantities to provide saw logs for mills running out of white pine. As the last of the Arrowhead pine fell, there were too few maples to build businesses, and the trees were of no use to the pulp cutters who succeeded the lumbermen of the white pine era. The slow-growing broadleafs and their aspen and birch cousins now dominate the land of the pineries. In their own way, the maples are as magical as the pines. They have lived through everything since the Civil War. Like all the slower-growing broadleaf species, the hardest of the hardwoods, their numbers have been sharply reduced, but they are not the object of reverence. The forest service has no signs telling us their age.

The climax maple forest is, in fact, parklike; more or less what the woods by grandmother's house are supposed to look like. The trees do have some use. Maple sugar amateurs trying to re-create a sense of contact with their past, with the woods, can bleed their sap to sweeten cakes, to make candies and syrups. The broadleafs simply get on better with modern man. Stop under the trees, peel back layer after layer of fallen leaves, and read the dominance of the maples in inches of compacted leaves pressed into soil by their own accumulation. These are the trees we have helped to win. They bless us with an annual glory of red or gold. They've been cut into oblivion by our brothers and sisters elsewhere in the world, but here in our part of the world, on their hillside, there are no questions. We are companions in the conquest of the pines. Maples too can provide a sustained yield.

As time passed, we did try to make peace with the pine. As early as 1860, Lake States residents and lawmakers began raising questions about preserving forests and saving some of the pine; and when the pine were nearly gone, various groups and agencies tried to reforest the cutovers in Michigan, Wisconsin, and Minnesota to save some of the land so that the pine could return. In small ways, they've had some successes, saved some pines, reseeded some. But the broadleafs have more agents than man. And no species controls as much as it might seem to.

Travel on. Back to the truck trail. North and east to Finland, Minnesota. Follow Lake County 7 north and east out of Finland, up the valley of the east branch of the Baptism, past the headwaters of the Caribou to Nine Mile Lake. Turn due east on Forest Road 166 to the Sawbill Trail. There find the Blister Rust Research Station. Not only did the Europeans bring the ax, the crosscut saw, the rails, and the way of steel to the pineries, they brought their flora and fauna, their science. As the century turned, Gifford Pinchot, America's first secretary of the interior, brought a new science from the Old World. Europe had come to treasure its woodlands, and forestry was born. And so it came to pass that the "trees of Carmenia" mingled with the trees of the Old Northwest as man sought to perfect and conserve. Conservation was born to save and restore what seemed to be passing. The foresters brought the trees of the Old World to perfect the trees of the new. With the trees came spores, a fungus. The winds blew. Spores floated, dropped on broadleaf gooseberries and currants, waited for the change that would make them ready for the pine, floated again on the helping wind, and the pine seedlings of the New World met a disease of the old. There is a sign explaining it all at the Blister Rust Research Station. The foresters of the station are trying to develop rust-resistant pines. *Rust-resistant* — the phrase rings of metal but speaks of spores. Think back to the Copper Tree of Pine City, to the white pine as boundary, to rows of red pine along the highways, the changing of the guard, bugs, men, trees; atoms dancing, flickering into new shapes. And the pines had dominion, and then there were flowers, and then there was humankind, and then there was steel, and then there was steam and cities. Man and woman came to dominion, and now the New World is theirs. The trees contained the human community. The human community contains the trees.

The only lesson to be learned from this is the lesson that all history, philosophy, religion, and science teaches. While there are many ways to read the evolution of the human species, at least this much seems clear: in the process of becoming self-conscious, humankind created in itself a sense of choice and a sense of responsibility for actions taken. We have recently come to a point where we talk of our responsibilities to defend the rights of people very different from ourselves and debate questions about human rights and our responsibility to seek for others what we want for ourselves.

The time is at hand to look beyond our species, recog-

nizing our community with aspen, birch, pine, oak, and maple, with the microscopic flora and fauna that make soil, perhaps with the rocks themselves. And we have. Courts of law have debated the rights of snail darters and whales. The Supreme Court of the United States has argued cases involving the rights of ecosystems. Christopher Stone argues the case in *Should Trees Have Standing*, a legal brief claiming that natural objects ought to be granted status in the courts as holders of legal rights. He says, "The Court may be at its best in summoning up from the human spirit the kindest most generous and worthy ideas that abound there, giving them shape and reality and legitimacy. . . . And in the case of the environment the Supreme Court may find itself in a position to award 'rights' in a way that will contribute to a change in popular consciousness." Such changes do occur. We continue to debate such questions because we've slowly come to see this planet as an organism, a living thing, a cell whose parts are interdependent. We'll argue about acid rain and what it's doing to fish, water, and trees, about nuclear power and bombs, about developing or conserving, about living and dying. Such is the way of consciousness.

The white pines have passed. To blame is pointless, to praise meaningless. The world we live in was dreamed by Weyerhaeuser, Rockefeller, Hill, my father, your mother, you and I. The immigrants have been coming for nearly six hundred years, are still coming, still seeking, still hoping for a better tomorrow. Such is the way of humankind and, hence, of this planet. We need not accept any particular explanations or justifications. Ask not if it was Yaweh, Allah, God, a random combination of molecules, the big bang. Accept the miracle of rocks, fluids, and gases springing to life, of life becoming sentient, of sentience becoming awareness. Even if this is all passing, it is glorious. Love all the things around you. Lament the passing of the lordly pine but treasure the lowly aspen, its 30,000 years of root life reflowering in infinities of trees whose fibers house, heat, illuminate, educate. Treasure the red pine, the spruce, the tag alder, the willow, the tamarack, the cedar. These are the living woods with us this moment. We have evolved together. We share this space and time. What has been is not likely to be again, that is the way of evolution. The dance, so long as it lasts, will be to new forms. Some will survive, some will fail. At the moment when our remote ancestors stepped out onto the plain into consciousness, saw the world as it might be, and set out to make it over in their image, they also looked back in among the trees and lamented for what had passed, for it too had been good.

The Dead River Mill and Crew, Michigan, 1893. *Courtesy, Marquette County Historical Society.*

(Opposite page, top)
Unloading logs at the Paine Lumber Company sawmill in Oshkosh, Wisconsin. *Courtesy, Oshkosh Public Museum.*

(Opposite page, bottom)
Paine Lumber Company Mantel and Newel Department employees, 1899. *Courtesy, Oshkosh Public Museum.*

First mills built at Minneapolis, Minnesota in 1859. The first sawmill was erected on what was later known as the platform where nearly all the sawmills were massed at a later period. *Courtesy, Minnesota Historical Society*.

(Opposite page)
Virgin white pine in Wisconsin. *Courtesy, State Historical Society of Wisconsin*.

A sketch of the Walker, Judd and Veazie sawmill at Marine Mills, Minnesota on the St. Croix River. This mill, the first in the state, was built in 1839 and was operated by water, by means of a flutter whell, later changed to an overshot whell with buckets. *Courtesy, Minnesota Historical Society. Photo: John Runk.*

Schomer and Gallagher Sawmill at Noray, Wisconsin, 1882. *Courtesy, Oshkosh Public Museum.*

Logs stockpiled outside the sawmills in Duluth, Minnesota. circa 1890's. *Courtesy, NE Minnesota Historical Center.*

(Opposite page, top)
Log mill pond and slip in Michigan, 1896.

(Opposite page, bottom)
Maple logs to be sawed for flooring lumber are stored awaiting their turn at the mill. *Courtesy, Wisconsin Land & Timber Company, Hermansville, Michigan.*

A view of the log pond and log slip at the David Tozer Company's sawmill on the St. Croix at South Stillwater, Minnesota. Many hundreds of millions of feet of logs of whitepine went up this log slip to be converted into high grade lumber, later shipped to all points of the world. *Courtesy, Minnesota Historical Society. Photo: John Runk.*

(Opposite page, top)
Sawmills along the Menominee River in Menominee, Michigan, 1898. *Courtesy, U.S. Library of Congress.*

(Opposite page, bottom)
The town of Emerson, Wisconsin and its sawmill in 1908. Many such towns grew up around a sawmill and were consequently abandoned when the sawmill closed. *Courtesy, State Historical Society of Wisconsin.*

127

Sawmill interior in International Falls, Minnesota. *Courtesy, Minnesota Historical Society.*

(Opposite page, top)
Issac Staples' St. Croix Mill with the Staples' residence in the background in 1880. *Courtesy, Minnesota Historical Society. Photo: John Runk.*

(Opposite page, bottom)
White pine logs measuring four to six feet across at an unidentified location in Minnesota. *Courtesy, Minnesota Historical Society.*

A waterboy at a lumbermill in Minnesota in 1890. There was always work for young boys around the mills. *Courtesy, Minnesota Historical Society.*

(Opposite page, top)
The first cut on a log in the sawmill. *Courtesy, Northeast Minnesota Historical Center.*

(Opposite page, bottom)
Illustration of a "gang saw" used in midwestern sawmills. These saws, while not widely used, cut complete logs into boards. This was a reciprocating saw and because it was slow and prone to breakdowns, fell into disuse. *Courtesy, Marquette County Historical Society.*

The interior of the Paine Lumber Company in Oshkosh, Wisconsin in the 1890's. At the time, this was one of the largest millworks for doors and windows in the world. *Courtesy, Oshkosh Public Museum.*

(Opposite page, top)
The interior of a sawmill shop. The bandsaw blades are mounted in special vises for the cleaning, filing and setting of teeth. *Courtesy, Marquette County Historical Society.*

(Opposite page, bottom)
Interior of the Paine Lumber Company, Oshkosh, Wisconsin in the 1890's. *Courtesy, Oshkosh Public Museum.*

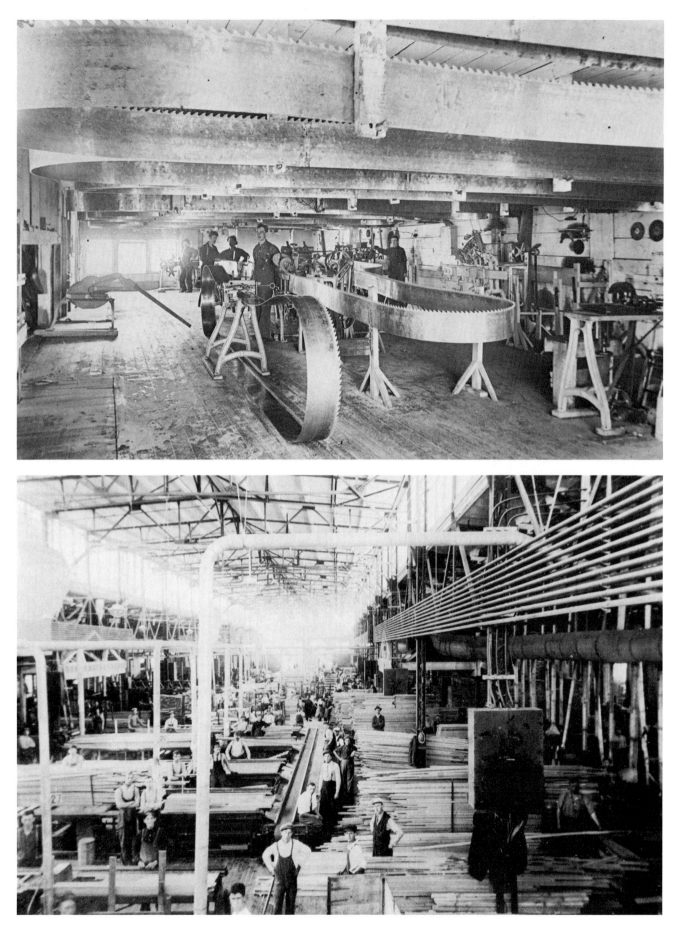

A 1930 photograph of a new sawmill and sorting shed in Cloquet, Minnesota. *Courtesy, Minnesota Historical Society.*

(Opposite page, top)
Lumber yard of the Hersey & Bean Lumber Company. This portion was built on pilings over the St. Croix River. The railroad tracks were for the Milwaukee Railroad in 1885. *Courtesy, Minnesota Historical Society.*

(Opposite page, bottom)
Portable sawmill on the Wolf River in Wisconsin in the 1890's. *Courtesy, Oshkosh Public Museum.*

A pile of some of the best pine lumber in Minnesota. This pile contains about 25,000 feet of
lumber which had been cut for Eastern markets. Sawed at Stillwater, Minnesota in 1912.
Courtesy, Minnesota Historical Society. Photo: John Runk.

(Opposite page)
Frank Stenlund, a lumber company employee, stands next to three foot wide white pine
boards in 1912. *Courtesy, Minnesota Historical Society. Photo: John Runk.*

A "Dry-pile" of cut lumber. *Courtesy, Wisconsin Land & Timber Company, Hermansville, Michigan.*

(Opposite page, top)
A Paine Lumber Company delivery wagon. *Courtesy, Oshkosh Public Museum.*

(Opposite page, bottom)
Guards at the Hermansville, Michigan mills during a loggers strike in 1916. *Courtesy, Wisconsin Land & Timber Company, Hermansville, Michigan.*

First Line of Defense

A lumber barge at the Albany Lumber Market. Much of the lumber cut in the northwoods from 1850 through 1920 was shipped east and sold to builders through the Albany and Tonawanda, New York markets. *Courtesy, Albany Institute of History and Art.*

(Opposite page)
The logger was frequently glamorized by eastern magazines. This example appeared in Harper's Magazine in the 1880's. *Courtesy, State Historical Society of Wisconsin.*

WISCONSIN — ON THE LUMBER DRIVE IN THE ST. CROIX.

Joe Mufraw was another comical character who grew out of advertising copy in the early 1900's. *Courtesy, State Historical Society of Wisconsin*.

Paul Bunyon and his blue ox, Babe. Although thought to be a folk creation of loggers' bunk-house and long winter nights, the Paul Bunyon myth was actually the fabrication of William B. Laughead, an advertising copywriter. Laughead wrote a collection of stories, featuring Paul Bunyon, which were sent to customers of the Red River Lumber Company in 1914. *Courtesy, State Historical Society of Wisconsin*.

Courtesy, Minnesota Historical Society.

Bibliography

The books, articles and maps that are listed below were invaluable aids in helping the author to develop an understanding of white pine logging in the Lake States. Without the work of the scientists, scholars and writers listed here this popular history of white pine logging could not have been written.

Billard, J. B. (ed.) *The World of the American Indian*. Washington: National Geographic, 1979.

Blair, W. A. *A Raft Pilot's Log*. Cleveland: Clark, 1930.

Conron, J. B. *The American Landscape*. New York: Oxford, 1973.

Dorson, R. M. *Bloodstoppers and Bear Walkers*. Cambridge: Harvard, 1952.

Edlin, H. and Nimmo, M. *The Illustrated Encyclopedia of Trees*. New York: Crown, 1978.

Finley, R. W. "Original Vegetation Cover of Wisconsin." (Map and Notes). St. Paul: U.S. Forest Service, 1976.

Fries, R. F. *Empire in Pine*. Madison: Historical Society, 1951.

Havighurst, W. *Upper Mississippi*. New York: Farrar and Rinehart, 1937.

Hidy, R. W., Hill, F. E. and Nevins, A. *Timber and Men*. New York: Macmillan, 1963.

Holbrook, S. H. *Holy Old Mackinaw*. New York: Macmillan, 1956.

Ketchum, R. *The Secret Life of the Forest*. New York: American Heritage, 1970.

Kümmerly, W. *The Forest*. Washington: Luce, 1973.

Larson, Agnes M. *History of the White Pine Industry in Minnesota*. Minneapolis: University of Minnesota, 1949.

Longyear, J. M. *Landlooker in the Upper Peninsula of Michigan*. St. Paul: Marquette County Historical Society, 1960.

Marscher, F. J. *Original Vegetation of Minnesota* (Map with Notes by Heinselman, M. L.) St. Paul: Forest Service, 1974.

Maybee, R. H. *Michigan's White Pine Era, 1840–1900*. Lansing: Michigan Department of State, 1976.

Meek, R. *Michigan's Timber Battleground*. Clave County: Bicentennial Historical Committee, 1976.

Morison, S. E. *The Oxford History of the American People*. New York: Oxford, 1965.

Neal, E. G. *Woodland Ecology*. London: Heineman, 1958.

Peattie, D. C. *Natural History of Trees of Eastern and Central United States*. Boston: Houghton-Mifflin, 1966.

Rector, W. G. *Log Transportation in the Lake States Lumber Industry, 1840–1918*. Glendale, California: Clark, 1953.

Sanford, A. H. and Hirshheimer, H. J. *A History of LaCrosse, Wisconsin, 1841–1900*. LaCrosse: County Historical Society, 1951.

Schultz, Rose (ed.) *Hermansville Centennial, 1878–1978*. Hermansville, Michigan: Centennial Committee, 1978.

Schwartz, G. M. and Thiel, G. A. *Minnesota's Rocks and Waters*. Minneapolis: University of Minnesota, 1963.

Sims, P. K. and Morey, G. B. (eds.) *Geology of Minnesota*. St. Paul: Minnesota Geological Survey, 1972.

Stone, C. D. *Should Trees Have Standing*. Los Altos, California: Kaufman, 1972.

Thoreau, H. D. *The Maine Woods*. Princeton, New Jersey: Princeton University, 1972.

Turner, F. W. *North American Indian Reader*. New York: Viking, 1974.

Willard, D. E. *The Story of the North Star State*. St. Paul: Webb, 1922.

Wright, H. E. "The Roles of Pine and Spruce in the Forest History of Minnesota and Adjacent Areas." *Ecology*, 1968, 49, 937–955.

Wright, H. E. and Frey, D. G. (eds.) *The Quaternary of the United States*. Princeton, New Jersey: Princeton University, 1965.

Wright, H. E. and Watts, W. A. *Glacial and Vegetational History of Northeastern Minnesota*. Minneapolis: University of Minnesota, 1969.

Glossary of Terms

band saw — a continuous band of toothed steel revolving around rotating drums.

Bangor Tigers — the shantyboys who logged in the Bangor area.

banking ground — an area adjacent to streams where logs were piled awaiting the spring drive.

bank scale — the estimate made by the scaler at the banking ground of the number of board feet in each log.

barker — a machine which removed bark from logs during the milling process.

bateau — a flat-bottom boat used to transport driving crews during river drives.

Big Wheels — a pair of large spoked wheels connected by an axle. The wheels were large enough to clear stumps and were used to haul logs to landings during the summer months.

birler — a boom worker or riverman whose job was to spin a floating log by taking small, rapid steps digging his calked boots into the log.

birling — spinning a floating log by taking a series of small, rapid steps digging the spikes of calked boots into the log.

blue — a log with a sharp taper so that the diameter of one end was visibly smaller than that of the other end.

board feet — a measure of the number of feet of lumber one inch thick and twelve inches (one foot) wide that could be cut from each log at the mills.

boiling up — a process used to launder the lumbermen's clothes while in camp. The clothes were literally boiled in a large tub.

boom — a line of logs chained together to contain other logs. The term also refers to the log-sorting yards that developed on major logging streams where a long string of chained logs was used to catch the logs being floated to the mills.

boomers — the men who worked at the log-sorting yards.

boom master — the supervisor who directed operations at the log-sorting booms.

boom stick — one of the logs in a line of chained logs.

boom works — the log-sorting yards on the major logging rivers.

breakup — the point in the spring of the year when the ice went out of lakes and streams.

breech-loader — a lumber camp bunk entered from the side.

bucking — sawing the felled trees into sixteen-foot logs.

bull chain — a heavy chain with teeth welded to it which pulled logs up from the millpond to the mill saws.

bull cook — the chore boy at late nineteenth century camps.

bunk — the wooden-framed, shelf-like structure on which the lumberjack slept.

calk — the spikes on the books which riverhogs wore.

cant — the angle at which a saw is set, or the log which has had bark slabs removed.

cant dog — a riverman's tool used to turn and maneuver logs consisting of a wooden handle with a sharp metal point and a free-swinging hook.

cant hook — a tool similar to the cant dog but shorter and without the sharp metal point used to load logs on sleighs.

capstan — a larger circular drum operated by hand or steam used on towboats to take up or slack off lines as rafts were steered through river channels.

catchmark — a mark in the end of the log made at the boom works to make log identification easier.

chainer — the man on a lumber crew responsible for chaining logs to the go-devil or sleighs.

chain saw — a gas-operated, hand-held power saw consisting of cutting teeth mounted on a chain which slides around a cutting bar.

chantey — a working man's song sung while working.

cheat stick — the measuring stick used to estimate the number of board feet in a log.

146

cookee — the cook's helper.

cordelling — walking along the shore pulling log and lumber rafts through waters where the current would not suffice and when sails could not be used.

cork log — white pine logs which despite size floated high in the water.

cracked stem — a broken arm or leg.

crossbar — a reinforcing piece of wood used to strengthen a go-devil.

crosscut saw — a saw designed to cut across the grain of the wood for felling trees.

cruiser — a woodsman who went out to locate and claim the stands of white pine and other types of trees for the lumber companies.

cut — the total number of trees felled, or the place where trees were being cut, or the actual groove being made by a saw.

cutoff saw — the saw that was used in the mills to trim the ends of boards or to cut them to desired lengths.

cutover — an area where all the desirable trees had been logged and where stumps and branches remained.

deacon's bench — the long bench in the camp bunkhouse where lumbermen sat in the evenings.

decker — a woods worker who helped to stack logs at landings or in the banking yard.

dog — the hook on cant hooks or cant dogs.

double gang — a large set of parallel saw blades used to saw logs into boards.

drive — the process of floating logs down streams from the woods to mills or booms.

dry kiln — a large shed that used steam heat for drying out lumber.

edger — a saw used for trimming the edges of boards.

edgerman — a millworker who operated the edger.

filer — a skilled lumber camp worker or millworker responsible for sharpening saws.

flaggins — a hot lunch delivered to lumber camp workers while they were in the woods working.

flume — a wooden chute made to carry logs around waterfalls.

gang edger — an edger with many blades capable of edging many boards at one time.

gang saw — a set of frame saws or gate saws operating in unison to saw a log into boards.

gate saw — a saw blade set in a frame that was moved up and down by waterpower.

glim — the single lamp that was used to light early lumber camps.

go-devil — a wishbone-shaped tree crotch that was used to haul bucked logs to landings or banking yards.

groundhog — a man who used cant hooks to roll logs up onto sleighs or railcars.

gummed — the result of failing to keep both ends of a log even when rolling it into place on a sleigh or railcar.

gyppo — a lumberman who worked on a contract basis.

hayman-on-the-hill — a woods worker who threw hay on ice-road downhill grades to slow loaded sleighs so they would not overrun the horses pulling them.

headwater — the source of a stream or river.

headworks — a raft with a hand- or horse-powered windlass used to tow rafts across lakes.

ice road — a road made by cutting grooves in the snow with a rut cutter and then icing the grooves.

inkslinger — the lumber camp clerk.

jam — a pile up of logs during the river drive.

jam crew — the crews that worked to break up log jams.

jammer — a cranelike device for loading logs on to railcars, first powered by horses and later by steam.

jobber's sun — the moon. Contract lumbermen, or jobbers, worked to meet delivery quotas and deadlines, sometimes having to work by moonlight.

junk wagon — the wagon used to bring lunch to a woods crew.

kerf — the cut made by a saw.

king log — the central log in a log jam. Once loosened, the jam would break.

landing — any area where logs were piled.

landing man — a man who worked piling logs at a landing.

landlooker — the same as a cruiser.

limbing — cutting the branches off freshly felled trees.

loader — a man responsible for loading logs on sleighs or railcars.

loading gang — the group of men responsible for loading logs on sleighs or railcars.

logger — a term now used to refer to all woods workers. In the days of white pine lumbering, the term was used to refer to those who cut trees for uses other than making lumber. Such workers were considered to be the inferiors of lumbermen.

log-hauler — a steam tractor capable of pulling several logging sleighs.

lugs — the teeth on a bull chain that caught logs and pulled them into the mills.

lumberjack — the term applied to white pine woods workers in the Lake States region.

lumberman — a general term applied to all those involved in the production of white pine lumber.

mackinaw — a heavy woolen coat worn by lumberjacks and shantyboys.

man catcher — a recruiter for the lumbering camps.

millrace — the waterway used to divert water to turn mill wheels.

millwright — a builder of mills and mill machinery.

muley saw — an early improvement of the gate saw.

muzzleloader — a bunk that had to be entered from the end.

off-bearers — the millhands who carried away finished lumber.

outfitting operation — the preparations to send a crew into the woods.

peatland — a mixed coniferous forest land area which is characterized by peat bogs.

peavey — a name for cant dogs and cant hooks drawn from the name of its inventor.

pinery — the area of the forest containing red and white pine.

pit saw — the earliest form of saw for making lumber. It was operated by two men, one of whom stood in a pit. Each board was separately sawed.

poling — pushing logs or rafts along with a long, slender pole.

pulper — a logger who cut pulpwood for paper mills.

pulpwood — wood used in making paper.

rigging gang — the crew that loaded freshly cut logs onto sleds.

ripsaw — a saw for cutting boards to narrower widths.

river driver — a worker on logging river drives.

riverhog — another name for river drivers.

riverman — a worker on the log or lumber rafts and another name for river drive workers.

road monkey — a lumber crew member responsible for building and maintaining logging roads.

rollway — a steep bank along a stream where logs were rolled into the stream.

round turn — the area used to turn sleighs around at the banking yard.

run — to move along the shore with the first logs of the river drive.

rut cutter — a special sleigh that cut grooves on ice roads.

sacking — following the river drive and breaking loose stranded logs by standing in the water and twisting logs loose with the cant dog.

Saginaw — using the cant hook to retard the large end of a blue in loading a sleigh.

sash saw — the same as the gate saw.

saw filer — a man who sharpened saws by filing.

sawmill — the place where logs are sawed to make lumber.

sawyer — a saw operator.

scaler — a man responsible for estimating the number of board feet of lumber in a log.

scaling — estimating the number of board feet in a log.

shantyboy — an early name for a man who felled the white pine.

shantyman — an alternative form of shantyboy, sometimes used to refer to a member of the raft crews who lived in small shanties on the early rafts.

skidder — a device for moving logs from the place where they were cut to loading decks.

skidway — a narrow trail along which logs were pulled to the loading decks.

sky hooker — a man who worked placing logs on top of the loads when logs were being loaded on sleighs or railcars.

sled tender — a man who worked loading and helping to maneuver sleds.

slough — a swamp or river backwater.

sluice gate — a gate for releasing water into a millrace or flume.

snoose — snuff.

snubber — a device for braking sleighs on steep grades.

St. Croix — using the cant hook to speed the small end of a blue in loading a sleigh.

stagged overalls — overalls cut off at knee length to avoid having them catch on floating logs.

steam jammer — a steam-operated jammer.

steam nigger — a device for turning logs at the sawmill to position them properly for sawing.

stumpage — the fee paid for the standing trees that are part of a particular stand that is to be cut, or the trees themselves.

swamper — a lumber crewman responsible for clearing skidways.

teamster — the driver of teams of oxen or horses.

tie hacker — a logger who cut trees for railroad ties.

timber cruiser — the same as cruiser and landlooker.

timberman — a general term like lumberman.

top loader — the same as sky hooker.

traces — the harness used on horses.

tramway — a rail and cart system for carrying lumber to the drying yards.

turkey — the sack in which the early lumbering crews carried their individual possessions and clothing.

tussock — another name for the turkey.

undercutting — making a cut on the side of the tree opposite the main cut which determines where the tree will fall.

walking the cook — stopping work to protest bad food or cooking.

wanigan — the supply store at a camp, or the floating, sleeping, and cooking quarters on a river drive.

whipsaw — the same as a pit saw.

white water man — another name for a river driver.

winch — a device used for hoisting heavy loads.

windfall — a tree blown over by the wind.

windlass — a device used for hauling or lifting.

yardmaster — the man in charge of a lumber yard.

Notes

Page 2

Bedagi, or Big Thunder, was a Wabakanis, an alliance of five tribes located along the Kennebec River in Maine. He made this statement at the turn of the century. The quotation can be found on page 22 of *Touch the Earth*, a collection of Native American statements about people and nature compiled by T. C. McLuhan and published by E. P. Dutton and Company, New York, in 1972.

This Winnebago saying is a "commonplace," a piece of conventional wisdom passed from generation to generation by word of mouth. It is also contained in McLuhan's *Touch the Earth* on page 5.

Tatanga Mani, or Walking Buffalo, was a member of a northern plains tribe which lived on both sides of the border between the United States and Canada in the Montana region. His words are also included in McLuhan's *Touch the Earth* on page 23.

Anaguoness, an Ojibway (Chippewa), was wounded serving with the Allied Forces in World War I. The quotation is part of a letter written to his nurse. The entire letter can be found in *I Have Spoken*, a collection of Native American speeches and writings edited by Virginia L. Armstrong and published by the Swallow Press, Inc., in Chicago during 1971. The selection appears on pages 141 to 144.

Page 2

Governor Bradford's words are from *Of Plymouth Plantation*, his account of the history of the first New England colony written in 1630. This quotation can be found on page 118 of John Conron's anthology *The American Landscape*, published by Oxford University Press in New York during 1973.

Page 10

Stuart Holbrook's *Holy Old Mackinaw* is a well written and interesting account of white pine lumbering. Holbrook manages to be both humorous and accurate. These words can be found on page 78 of his book, originally published in 1956 by the Macmillan Company of New York.

Page 10

Hector St. Jean Crevecoeur, an early French immigrant to the American colonies, wrote his observations shortly after the Revolutionary War. The section of his *Letters from an American Farmer* can be found in Conron's anthology on page 132.

Page 13

Henry David Thoreau's comments on Bangor are made in *The Maine Woods* and can be found on page 82 of the Princeton University Press edition published at Princeton, New Jersey, in 1972.

Page 13

Holbrook writes about the history of Bangor, Maine, on pages 14 through 40 of his *Holy Old Mackinaw*. These specific statements are on pages 22 and 28.

The remarks of the New York businessman George Titus can be found on page 51 of Forrest Meek's *Michigan's Timber Battleground*, published by the Clare County Bicentennial Historical Committee in 1976.

Page 15

Agnes Larson's *History of the White Pine Industry in Minnesota* is one of the most thoroughly researched and detailed histories of white pine lumbering ever written. Much of the factual information in this book is drawn from Ms. Larson's extraordinary work. She discusses the sale of these pinelands on page 252 of her book which was published by the University of Minnesota Press in Minneapolis during 1949.

Page 15

Daniel Stanchfield's timber cruising is discussed on page 169 of Ms. Larson's history of white pine lumbering.

Page 17

The description of Al Nason is from Ms. Larson's history. It can be found on pages 172 and 173.

Page 49

Daniel Stanchfield is quoted in Ms. Larson's book on page 169.

Page 50

The "Song of the Western Pioneer" is reprinted on pages 83 to 84 in Ms. Larson's history. It was written by Dillon O'Brien and first appeared in the *Stillwater Messenger*, June 5, 1867.

Page 52

The description of the attire of raft pilots is from Ms. Larson's history. It can be found on page 90.

Page 52–53

These comments on the perils of rafting can be found on page 87 of Ms. Larson's book and are drawn from the papers of Franklin Steele.

Page 78

Ms. Larson reports the lumber camp poets description of waking up on page 195 of her book. It originally appeared in the *Minneapolis Tribune* for February 20, 1875.

Page 79

The first two choruses of lumberjack songs are found in Walter Havighurst's wilderness saga *Upper Mississippi*, published by Farrar and Rinehart of New York in 1937. The song is found on page 171.

Swan Swanson's song is found on page 172 of Havighurst's book.

The song of Louie Sands and Jim McGee is from page 9 of Roland Maybee's pamphlet on Michigan lumbering, *Michigan's White Pine Era*, published by the Michigan History Division, Michigan Department of State at Lansing, Michigan, in 1976.

The chorus from the raftsmen's song is from Holbrook's *Holy Old Mackinaw*, page 138.

The song of the Kettle River lumbermen is from Ms. Larson's history and can be found on page 203. It was sung to Mr. O'Brien by John Stewart, age 88.

The last two choruses of lumberjack music are from "The Lumberjack" which, according to Ms. Larson on page 205, was first printed in the Bemidji Daily Pioneer in March of 1914.

Page 80

Ms. Larson tells the story of the lonely young jack on page 209 of her book.

Page 80

Moonlight Harry Schmidt's account of lumberjacks is from page 187 of Richard Dorson's *Blood Stoppers and Bear Walkers*, a collection of folk tales published by Harvard University Press at Cambridge, Massachusetts, in 1952.

The Iron County jack's story can be found on page 187 of Dorson's book.

Page 81

Dorson's stories of fights and barroom chants are told on pages 188 to 194 of his book.

Page 83

Ms. Larson discusses driving companies on page 187 of her history.

Page 83

Ben Harcourt's description of log drives is taken from pages 29 to 34 of Roland Maybee's pamphlet on Michigan lumbering.

Page 84

Otis Terpening's lines come from "The River Drivers Grave," a poem in the Charles E. Brown papers, which are held by the Wisconsin Historical Society. They appear on pages 188 to 189 of Ms. Larson's book.

Page 84

The description of a typical boom can be found on pages 128 and 129 of William G. Rector's *Log Transportation in the Lake States*, published by Arthur H. Clarke Company at Glendale, California, in 1953.

Page 84

The description of log sorting can be found in Rector's work on log transportation on pages 134 and 135.

Page 84

The description of the process of making log rafts can be found on page 152 of Rector's book.

Page 85

Ms. Larson describes the steam nigger on page 147 of her history.

Page 87

Ms. Larson discusses Crookston's wheat and lumber history on page 157 of her book.

Page 87

William Rector describes theenormous pile of wood on the frozen Mississippi on page 228 of his book on log and lumber transportation.

Page 117

Christopher Stone is a lawyer. His argument is contained in *Should Trees Have Standing*, a legal brief printed originally in and cited by Justice Douglas in writing his opinion on the case of the *Sierra Club vs. Morton, Secretary of the Interior, et al.*, a suit brought by the Sierra Club on behalf of the ecosystem for the Mineral King Valley. This portion of the argument appears on page 53 of Stone's brief which was reprinted by William Kaufman, Inc., of Los Altos, California, in 1974.